BECOMING A WOMAN OF WISDOM

Crossway books by Joyce Rogers

The Bible's Seven Secrets to Healthy Eating
Becoming a Woman of Wisdom

BECOMING A
WOMAN OF WISDOM

Joyce Rogers

CROSSWAY BOOKS • WHEATON, ILLINOIS
A DIVISION OF GOOD NEWS PUBLISHERS

Becoming a Woman of Wisdom

Copyright © 2001 by Joyce Rogers

Published by Crossway Books
       a division of Good News Publishers
       1300 Crescent Street
       Wheaton, Illinois 60187

Portions of this book were previously published as *The Secret of a Woman's Influence* (1988) and *The Wise Woman* (1980), both by Broadman Press.

Cover design: Uttley/DouPonce DesignWorks

Cover photo: Digital Stock

First printing 2001

Printed in the United States of America

Library of Congress Cataloging-in-Publication Data

Rogers, Joyce.
    Becoming a woman of wisdom / Joyce Rogers.
      p.   cm.
    Includes bibliographical references.
    ISBN 1-58134-249-7 (trade pbk. : alk. paper)
    1. Women—Religious life. 2. Wisdom (Biblical personification)
3. Christian life. I. Title.
BV4527 .R635   2001
. 248.8'43—dc21   2001001914
                                                CIP

15	14	13	12	11	10	09	08	07	06	05	04	03	02	01
15	14	13	12	11	10	9	8	7	6	5	4	3	2	1

The secret of a woman's influence is not equality or self actualization but a gracious acceptance of a divine assignment in the created order of things. Joyce Rogers's voice needs to be heard, articulating ancient principles given for the true liberation of both men and women.

-ELISABETH ELLIOT

This book is dedicated to my family.

First of all to Mother and Daddy, Guston and Gladys Gentry,
who first loved me and introduced me to the things of the Lord.

To my husband's parents, Rose and Arden Rogers,
who loved me like their own.

To my loving husband,
whose life and courageous preaching of the Word of God
have influenced and blessed my life more than any other person.

To my two daughters, Gayle and Janice,
who are like "cornerstones, polished after the similitude of a palace"
(Psalm 144:12).

To my two sons, Steve and David,
who are like "plants, grown up in their youth"
(Psalm 144:12).

To my eight grandchildren—
Renae, Angie, Rachel, Michael, Adrian, Jonathan, Andrew, and Stephen—
who are such a joy!

Contents

Personal Note to Readers

I suppose the greatest concept in living the Christian life is "balanced living." We are all tempted to get sidetracked on our own experience-oriented detours and place too much emphasis on one part or another of our Christian lives.

This book is not mere theory. It contains principles and illustrations tried in the crucible of real life. I believe with the "preacher" of Ecclesiastes that there is "a time to be born and a time to die . . . a time to weep and a time to laugh . . . a time to keep silence and a time to speak" (Eccl. 3:2, 4, 7). I hope these pages will help you achieve that balance in your own life.

I believe there should not be a definite division between the practical and the profound, the natural and the supernatural. As Oswald Chambers says, God's presence in our lives will make us "supernaturally natural and naturally supernatural."

Admittedly, this book is written from the perspective of a married woman. It is home-centered, family-centered, because this has been the sphere to which God has called me to "work out" my salvation. That doesn't mean I think it is God's will for every woman to marry. God leads some to the high calling of singleness. I trust that even those who are single will find help and blessing in this book.

I have written this book to show the secret of a woman's influence and authority in her Christian life. I have endeavored to examine how this influence is rooted in the Word of God, the Bible—the reliable written Word of God—and Jesus Christ—the trustworthy living Word of God. We will look at Jesus, our supreme example of equality of worth and submission to divine authority.

The extent and sphere of a wise woman's ministry are dependent upon ministering under authority and with the proper priority. I will differentiate between the priorities of the married woman and the single woman, while emphasizing the priorities of homemaking and motherhood.

Our study will show that rather than being oppressive, God's plan for women holds the secret to true fulfillment and the wise use of our talents, spiritual gifts, and influence.

And so, let's prayerfully embark on this exciting adventure to find God's plan for each of our lives.

—Joyce

PART ONE

Essentially Wise

1

Search for a Wise Woman

I applied mine heart to know, and to search, and to seek out
wisdom. . . . Behold, this have I found, saith the preacher,
counting one by one, to find out the account: Which yet my soul
seeketh, but I find not: one man among a thousand have I
found; but a woman among all those have I not found.

ECCLESIASTES 7:25A, 27-28 (KJV)

What an indictment! The preacher of Ecclesiastes was on a treasure hunt, searching for a wise person. He could not find even one woman in a thousand who sought after wisdom.

As I read these words over and over again, I asked, "Lord, could you find one wise woman in a thousand *today?*" I know some women who would fit into this category, but they are far too few.

I wanted to be the kind of woman God could count on—a God-fearing woman, full of wisdom. I wanted to let God take control of my life, and so I prayed:

Today and forever, Lord,
I'm letting You
be God in me—
in action!

I'm bowing out, and
I'm letting You bow in.
I'm going to let You

think through my mind,
react through my emotions, and
make decisions through my will.

Here, Lord, my body is available to You.
I've tried so many times
in my own strength
to be like You—to copy,
to imitate the good I saw in You;
But I'm finished with that now!

Come, take control of my life—
I want to be available, dear Jesus,
To be what You want me to be
And do what You want me to do!

Some people see wisdom as the ability to meet and evaluate the circumstances of life from their natural minds and experiences. The dictionary defines wisdom as "knowledge practically applied to the best ends; natural sagacity; prudence; skill in affairs; piety." These definitions appear to be good, but they are incomplete, for they approach the subject from a worldly perspective only.

God's wisdom is what we desperately need. Life is too complicated to try to make sense of circumstances from a human perspective. Only God's point of view is important. God's wisdom is the only true wisdom. "For My thoughts are not your thoughts, nor are your ways My ways, says the LORD. For as the heavens are higher than the earth, so are My ways higher than your ways, and My thoughts than your thoughts" (Isaiah 55:8-9).

WISE CHOICES

Life is made up of both time and judgment. Every moment we must decide how we will use our time. Every day we must choose what is right. For these choices we need wisdom.

Multitudes of projects clamor for my time. Some are good and some are bad. Some are in-between. I need more than my own wisdom to determine *what* to do and *when* to do it.

As a woman of God, I want to discern God's will. Nevertheless, life is sometimes confusing. A multitude of "good things" calls for my attention; one activity might be best at one time but not at another. Resting in the hammock might be best today but wrong tomorrow. How can I know where my priorities ought to be?

My judgment is needed in other circumstances as well. For example, does this scenario sound familiar? Brother is watching television. He walks out of the room. Sister comes in. She sees no one around and changes the channel. She is absorbed in another show when Brother comes back into the room. He says, "I was here first!" Sister replies, "You left the room. I'm not changing the channel. Mother!"

Who is right, and who is wrong? How will I resolve the conflict?

Multiply this scene by five family members, each with demands upon my time, opinions, and attention. How can I discover what I should do? The phone is ringing; my lost neighbors are silently calling; the church is beckoning; my community and school are begging me to respond to their needs. I need wisdom far beyond my own. Ecclesiastes 8:5b-6a says, "A wise man's heart discerns both time and judgment. Because for every matter there is a time and judgment."

How and where will we find the wisdom we need? First, we must desire it with all our hearts. Then, like the writer of Ecclesiastes, we must seek it diligently. "I applied my heart to know, to search and seek out wisdom" (7:25).

The Bible pictures wisdom as a hidden treasure: "My son, if you receive my words, and treasure my commands within you, So that you incline your ear to wisdom, and apply your heart to understanding; Yes, if you cry out for discernment, and lift up your voice for understanding, If you seek her as silver, and search for her as for hidden treasures; Then you will understand the fear of the LORD, and find the knowledge of God. For the LORD gives wisdom" (Prov. 2:1-6a).

We have a map to this treasure. It is God's Word. Join me in this search for the greatest treasure in the world—godly wisdom.

THE COMPANIONS OF WISDOM

Most people seek happiness. They capture it for a moment, only to have it slip through their fingers. They wonder where it hides and how they can own it. The Bible says that when we find wisdom, we will stumble across happiness along the way.

Happy is the man who finds wisdom, and the man who gains understanding; For her proceeds are better than the profits of silver, and her gain than fine gold. She is more precious than rubies, and all the things you may desire cannot compare with her. Length of days is in her right hand, in her left hand riches and honor. Her ways are ways of pleasantness, and all her paths are peace. She is a tree of life to those who take hold of her, and happy are all who retain her. (Prov. 3:13-18)

According to this passage, long life will be in wisdom's right hand and riches and honor in her left. Along this path we will also meet two more of wisdom's companions—pleasantness and peace. Indeed, these are the lasting treasures for which our hearts long. Aren't these treasures worth more than silver, gold, or precious jewels?

The other day a magazine caught my eye. On it was the picture of a striking woman with this provoking question underneath: "What makes a woman beautiful?" I want to be beautiful, so I read on. These items were listed—hairstyling, makeup, voice and diction, wardrobe, visual poise, social graces, personality development, figure.

I need all the help I can get in these areas. All these are important in making a woman *outwardly* beautiful. But as I pondered the list, I grew aware that something was missing. The article did not mention one word about inner beauty, demonstrated by wisdom, and how I could attain it.

To become *outwardly* beautiful I need expert counseling. I need to know what hairstyle is most becoming to me. I need to know what colors look best on me. I need to know my flaws and how to compensate for them. Only the more well-to-do can afford the costly services of a beauty consultant or fashion expert who can give instruction in these areas. (Do-it-yourself helps never seem to measure up to professional care.)

Inner beauty helps are quite the same. There are lots of do-it-yourself books, but they will never measure up to expert counseling. This professional help, however, is free of charge.

The Holy Spirit of God is the great inner-beauty consultant. His beauty manual is the Bible. It is illustrated with pictures of Jesus from Genesis to Revelation. The more we look at these pictures, the more we will be willing to forfeit earthly treasures to wear Jesus' likeness.

The Holy Spirit compares us to Jesus in order to make us dissatisfied with what we are. He knows that in our own strength the goal is impossible. Can you hear Him saying, "You cannot do it—but *I* can if you will just let Me?" One of the chief facets of real beauty is God's wisdom shining through.

What does this wisdom-graced inner beauty look like? I saw it reflected in my mother. She was more interested in my making the Lamb's Book of Life than the social register. Mother never taught me how to pour tea from a silver service, but she showed me the importance of the water of life. Though she never attended a Bible school, she studied the Bible in depth. To enhance my inner beauty, she directed me to read many books written by some of the greatest Christians of all time. She reminded me of the proverb, "Charm is deceitful and beauty is passing, but a woman who fears the Lord, she shall be praised" (31:30).

Conversely, one day God will reveal the shallowness of the world of fashion and flair. The inner ugliness of the worldly woman will then show through. Her weak points will be magnified. She will cry, embarrassed and ashamed. Everyone will know the truth that she tried to hide with mascara and makeup. For those overly proud of their good looks, God has in store a reverse treatment. Such was the fate of the "haughty daughters of Zion." Read about it in Isaiah 3:16-26 (TLB):

> *Next, he will judge the haughty Jewish women, who mince along, noses in the air, tinkling bracelets on their ankles, with wanton eyes that rove among the crowds to catch the glances of the men. The Lord will send a plague of scabs to ornament their heads! He will expose their nakedness for all to see. No longer shall they tinkle with self-assurance as they walk. For the Lord will strip away their artful beauty and their ornaments, their necklaces and bracelets and veils of shimmering gauze.*
>
> *Gone shall be their scarves and ankle chains, headbands, earrings, and perfumes; their rings and jewels, and party clothes and negligees and capes and ornate combs and purses; their mirrors, lovely lingerie, beautiful dresses and veils. Instead of smelling of sweet perfume, they'll stink; for sashes they'll use ropes; their well-set hair will all fall out; they'll wear sacks instead of robes. All their beauty will be gone; all that will be left to them is shame and disgrace. Their husbands shall die in battle; the women, ravaged, shall sit crying on the ground.*

WISE WOMEN DO NOT FEAR

Before we can pursue the path of the wise woman, we must find a starting place. The Bible says, "The fear of the LORD is the beginning of knowledge" (Prov. 1:7). So our search will begin with a healthy understanding of what it means to fear God and how He responds to those who fear Him.

The Bible commands us: "Do not fear" (Luke 12:7). First Peter 3:6 (NIV) admonishes us, "Do not give way to fear." Why, then, does Proverbs 31:30 say, "A woman who fears the LORD, she shall be praised"? Don't we have enough fears without acquiring another one?

Many a life is controlled, or is out of control, as the case may be, by reason of fear. We are fearful that friends will fail us. We are fearful that sickness will come, bringing hardship. We are fearful that we cannot hold out. We are fearful that our national mistakes will catch up with us. We are fearful that our personal mistakes will be our ruin. On every side we are surrounded by fears. [1] *(Dr. Paul Adolph)*

Fear may produce severe emotional tension and disease. Anxiety and worry are forms of fear that focus on situations that may never come to pass.

And yet God's secret of security is in fear—one particular fear, and only one. This one fear overcomes all other fears. "The secret of the LORD is with those who fear Him, and He will show them His covenant" (Ps. 25:14). The command to fear God permeates the Scriptures.

The LORD takes pleasure in those who fear Him, in those who hope in His mercy. (Ps. 147:11)

Let us hear the conclusion of the whole matter: fear God and keep His commandments, for this is man's all. (Eccl. 12:13)

Nor be afraid of their threats, nor be troubled. The LORD of hosts, Him you shall hallow; let Him be your fear, and let Him be your dread. He will be as a sanctuary, but a stone of stumbling and a rock of offense to both the houses of Israel, as a trap and a snare to the inhabitants of Jerusalem. (Isa. 8:12b-14a)

Let us have grace, by which we may serve God acceptably with reverence and godly fear. (Heb. 12:28)

Fear God and give glory to Him. (Rev. 14:7)

What does it mean to fear God? According to the New Scofield Reference Bible, "It involves a reverential trust in God, accompanied by a hatred of evil." [2] Charles Haddon Spurgeon said, "Pay to Him humble, childlike reverence, walk in His laws, have respect to His will, tremble to offend Him, hasten to serve Him . . . . Fear God and nothing else."

One of God's object lessons to teach us how to fear Him is the father-child relationship. I had a deep, loving trust in my daddy. I did not want to disappoint him. I desired his approval. Because of the kind of father he was, he deserved my respect. I knew he was the head of our family. He was the one who provided food, shelter, and clothing for us. He was faithful and loving in all he did. I trusted him implicitly.

There was another side to my respect, however. To this day I would not think of being disrespectful to my father. I feared the consequences of saying or doing the wrong thing. It was enough for me to observe his displeasure with my brothers. I did not want to bring that displeasure on myself.

Most people do not fear God because they do not know what He is like. They visualize Him as an old grandfather, tottering around heaven. We need to realize that He is the thrice-holy God of Israel. He is omnipotent, omniscient, and omnipresent. He will not overlook sin. We should fear His displeasure. Hebrews 10:31 says, "It is a fearful thing to fall into the hands of the living God." To the unbelieving there is "a certain fearful expectation of judgment, and fiery indignation" (Heb. 10:27).

God's children who disobey Him also have something to fear. Although they will experience the mercy of God in relation to eternal punishment, they can look forward to the sure chastening of the Lord during this life. But God's chastening comes because He loves us. He wants us to share His holiness. He is making us into His image through His corrective measures (see Heb. 12:5-15).

The best word to describe God is not *love* or *mercy* (even though He is these) but *holiness*. Evil is the antithesis of holiness. If we are to be like Him, we must learn to hate evil. "Let us cleanse ourselves from all filthiness of the flesh and spirit, perfecting holiness in the fear of God" (2 Cor. 7:1). How can we, who are deceitful and desperately wicked, discover the evil that lurks in our hearts? We must turn to the God of holiness and let Him reveal these hidden recesses. Oswald Chambers, who sought to be totally abandoned to God, wrote about holiness:

> The characteristic of the holiness of Almighty God is that it is absolute; it is impossible to antagonize or strain it. The characteristic of the holiness of Jesus is that it manifested itself by means of antagonism; it was a holiness that could be tested.
>
> The Son of God, as Son of Man, transformed innocence into holy character bit by bit as things opposed; He did not exhibit an immutable holiness but a holiness of which we can be partakers—"that we might be partakers of His Holiness" (Heb. 12:10). Jesus Christ revealed what a normal man should be and in so doing showed how we may become all that God wants us to be.[3]

God is loving, compassionate, and ready to forgive and provide for those who fear Him. Here are some of the promised provisions to those who fear God:

Strong confidence and a place of refuge (Prov. 14:26)
A fountain of life (Prov. 14:27)
Satisfaction (Prov. 19:23)
Riches and honor and life (Prov. 22:4)
A book of remembrance (Mal. 3:16)
A banner (Ps. 60:4)
His goodness (Ps. 31:19)
Will show His covenant (Ps. 25:14)
Prolonged days (Prov. 10:27)
Great mercy (Ps. 103:11)

The fear of God will be expressed both in our attitudes and in our actions. We will give honor to God through what we think, what we say, and what we do. The conclusion to what life is all about is expressed in Ecclesiastes 12:13: "Fear God and keep His commandments, for this is man's all."

2

The Wise Woman Works

Examine me, O LORD, and prove me;
try my mind and my heart.

PSALM 26:2

The path of self-analysis is barren! How often we have made New Year's resolutions, only to break them before the day is even over. How empty is our effort. We end up feeling guilty, and it seems that we were better off before we began to work on self-improvement. Seeking to change bad habits and character flaws is like peeling an onion. Underneath each layer of faults we find another layer that needs to change. What utter despair to see our failures and weaknesses and then be left without a solution. The Chinese Christian Watchman Nee said: "If all day long we analyze ourselves, dissecting our thoughts and feelings, it will hinder us from losing ourselves in Christ. Unless a believer is deeply taught by the Lord, he will not be able to know himself. Introspection and self-consciousness are harmful to spiritual life."[1]

On the other side of the coin is the self-righteous person who only becomes vain with self-analysis. I became a Christian when I was nine years old, and so I never tried many of the sins others indulged in. When the annual resolution time rolled around, my list of improvements was relatively short.

As the years hurried by, how God must have pitied me. I was only fooling myself. I had areas of my inner life that neither I nor others had ever really seen, but He was ever so patient with me. It was only through an hour of deep sorrow that I discovered the shallowness of my life. I began a diligent search to know God better. Through this search God led me to Psalm

139:23-24. I called out, "Search me, O God, and know my heart; try me, and know my anxieties; And see if there is any wicked way in me, and lead me in the way everlasting."

God alone can turn on the light within. I see only the outward issues, but God can see my attitudes and motives. God has 20/20 vision in the dark. When we ask, He turns on the searchlight so we can see our need of cleansing and renewal. His light comes to us in the form of His holy Word, which the Holy Spirit uses to help us see ourselves as He sees us.

IN FRONT OF GOD'S MIRROR

Examine me, O Lord, and prove me; try my mind and my heart. (Ps. 26:2)

Pick up the mirror of God's Word and take a look at yourself. Ask God's Holy Spirit to help you see the "real you." Each of us must deal with the sin question in a heart-searching manner before we are able to trust God with the rest of our lives. God must teach us to hate evil so that we might be free to love good.

Use the following as a guide:

Exam

(Check one or more as indicated)

I am
• a growing Christian.
• a backslidden Christian.
• not a Christian.

I spend the most time
• studying my Bible.
• reading the newspaper.
• reading secular magazines.
• other _____

I pray
• every day.
• sometimes.
• just in emergencies.
• other _____

I attend church
- two or more times a week.
- once a week.
- at least once a month.
- about twice a year.
- other _____

I give to the Lord
- a tenth and more of my income.
- a tenth of my income.
- whatever I feel I can afford.
- very little.
- other _____

I witness for the Lord
- whenever I find or can make opportunity.
- during revival meetings.
- hardly ever.
- never.
- other _____

I serve the Lord through the church
- in one or more capacities every week.
- whenever asked to do something special.
- never.
- other _____

I have
- no unconfessed sin in my life.
- at least one sin I refuse to confess.
- many sins in my life.

My husband and I pray together
- often.
- sometimes.
- seldom.
- never.

The following sins trouble me often:

- self pity
- argumentativeness
- pride
- impatience
- gluttony
- lust
- doubt

- gossip
- self-consciousness
- selfishness
- hatred
- jealousy
- lying
- exaggeration

- manipulation
- rebellion
- retaliation
- slothfulness
- resentment
- critical spirit
- other_____

I give priority to
- my husband and children over my own pursuits.
- to my separate vocation.

My time spent teaching my children spiritual things is
- adequate.
- not enough.
- not at all.

My husband and I discuss the Bible and spiritual things
- often.
- sometimes.
- seldom.
- never.

Our family has devotions together
- often.
- sometimes.
- seldom.
- never.

EVIDENCES OF A CHANGED LIFE

Let me share with you how the Holy Spirit's fullness changed my life as I began to look into the mirror of God's Word.

1. Jesus Christ became more real and precious than He had ever been before. I now had a desire to know Him—as He really is. My life became wonderful and exciting. I was always discovering new and glorious truths about Him. Fellowship with Him became sweet.

2. I did not become sinless, but a hunger for true holiness (the moral likeness of Jesus) was implanted within me. This involved so much more than my list of do's and don'ts. The Lord drew to my attention area after area in my life that I had barely noticed before. He showed me that I had been subconsciously proud of my own goodness and that it had made me intolerant of those who practiced the things that I did not do. He revealed to me my fear, lack of patience, and my self-pity. He showed me that I did not have His kind of love.

3. The devil became very real to me as I began to trust Christ for victory. He was not going to give up the fight easily. He tried to make my eyes dim and my ears dull to the fact that there is a life of victory. I discovered that when I trust Jesus, He does "battle" for me. His blood is sufficient for both my past sins and my present sins. I came to realize that Jesus can daily deliver me from sin because, "He always lives to make intercession for [me]" (Heb. 7:25b).

4. I realized that I had not been allowing Christ to control my life. I had been making my plans and asking God to bless them. He showed me that if I would just let Him be in control, I could live victoriously. One of the greatest truths I ever learned was that without Christ I am nothing. It was a hard lesson, for all my life my teachers and my friends had told me, "Joyce, you'll be something one day." He had to show me that the only way I could be anything was if He is everything. Norman Grubb put it this way, "Not to become something, but to contain Someone."

5. I began to talk to others about Jesus Christ. I had been able in my own strength to invite people to church and Sunday school, but talking to them about their personal experience with Jesus Christ scared me to death. I am still not all I should be in this area, but I praise Him that He showed me that I can't win people to Christ. Only the Holy Spirit can do that. I've learned to pray something like this, "Lord, You know what a coward I am, and I don't know what to say, but if You will just be with me and give me the words, I'll tell this person about Your love. I'm available, Lord. I'm trusting You to help me, for I know that You will not let me down." I've come away rejoicing from situations, knowing God spoke through me. Previously, I would not have had enough courage to say anything at all.

Perhaps your life has been like mine. If it has, I pray that these words might encourage you to "stop trying" to please God and "start trusting" Him for a life of victory.

Since I Thy love have known
Nought else can satisfy;
The fullness of Thy love alone
For this, for this, I cry.[2]

WORKING OUT WHAT GOD HAS WORKED IN

Some women are content to remain on the first basic level of Christian living. They are experience-oriented, thinking only about what God can do for them. They feel safe and secure just knowing that they are not going to hell.

From this level of the Christian life it is very easy to dart back and forth into worldly living. Since these women are "better" than worldly people, basic level Christians never see the need in their own lives. God may have to allow difficulties to come their way to show them their need for Him. If you are in this position, let me urge you to begin the adventure of "knowing Him."

This pursuit involves many levels of Christian living. The Holy Spirit becomes your personal guidance counselor. He is present at each new level, beckoning you on to new heights.

Discovery of truth is the means God uses to help you out of your difficulties and onto a new level of Christian living. God first enlightens your spirit with a new truth. Then your mind reasons it out. The truth seems to grip you as never before. You see an inner vision that is not your own. You will be so excited and eager to share your new insights, but there must be a time when you work out the reality of what God has worked in to your life.

PRACTICE MAKES PERFECT

God gives new revelations from His Word to your spirit, but you may have difficulty putting these new insights into practice in your daily life. Indeed there may be times of faltering and failing. Discovering spiritual truth and practicing spiritual truth are two different things. Therefore, when failures come, you may tend to doubt the reality of these truths.

You might turn aside, thinking God has failed. It is not God's failure, but your own misconception of what the Christian life is all about. Salvation is a reality, but there is still a lifetime of growth ahead of you. Proverbs 31:31 says that a woman's "own works praise her in the gates." A wise woman is diligently working out God's will in her life day by day, step by step.

ONLY A STEP

Only a step—
just one step
at a time.
Don't let me
walk ahead of You
nor linger far behind.
I look out far ahead
and cannot see;
Oh, Jesus Christ,
one step with You
is quite enough for me.

GOURMET LIVING

The apostle Paul didn't say to work for your salvation; rather he said, "work out your own salvation" (Phil. 2:12). You must possess salvation before you can work it out, just as you must have a food processor in your kitchen before you can assemble the finished product. Suppose you receive the gift of a new food processor and several bags of groceries. Together, this tool and these ingredients can create cakes, breads, puddings, soufflés, and more. But they don't do it on their own. You must do the work of combining the two to create these delicious delights that will satisfy your hunger.

In the same way, God gives us the gift of eternal life through His Son, Jesus Christ. That's His work—His alone. Our part as women in search of wisdom is to work this gift out in our own lives.

To continue the cooking analogy, as we practice cooking, our results will certainly improve. Our food simply tastes better after we've been cooking for years. We learn basic skills first. Then we experiment with simple recipes. Only then are we ready to proceed to entertain fifty guests for a gourmet dinner. We learn the skills of the Christian life just as we learn to cook—methodically, studiously, through much practice. As we practice, God will work into us continual gracious gourmet living.

Oswald Chambers explained it this way:

> The great need today among those of us who profess sanctification is the patience and ability to work out the holiness of God in every detail of the life. When we are first adjusted to God it is on the great big general lines; then the Holy Spirit educates us down to the scruples. He makes us sensitive to things we never thought of before.[3]

OUR PROBLEMS; GOD'S SOLUTIONS

We may have the right ingredients for a gourmet feast, but if our hands are dirty, the food will be contaminated with germs. The dirt can be visible to the naked eye, or it may be seen only through microscopic examination. Either way, it can poison good food.

At your current stage of spiritual life you may be appalled at the grosser sins such as adultery, stealing, and drunkenness. All these sins, however, have their beginning in more "respectable sins." You might even call them "bad attitudes." I will refer to them as "spiritual contaminants."[4] Examine with me a few of the contaminants that can defile the Christian woman as she works out her salvation.

Spiritual Contaminant—The Pollution of Perfectionism

I always wanted to be the "perfect" minister's wife. Anytime I heard someone say what a minister's wife ought to be or do, I made a mental note of it. After some years I had accumulated an impossible list.

Paul cautioned against the attitude of trying to be perfect according to this world's terms in the energy of the flesh. In Galatians 3:3 he writes, "Are you so foolish? Having begun in the Spirit, are you now being made perfect by the flesh?"

The perfectionist has an unbending attitude as she pursues perfection in her own strength. In her eyes this seems like a good quality; she usually does not recognize this trait as a serious source of tension in her life. Yet, taken to its extreme, perfectionism can result in a nervous breakdown, because no matter how much we try, our own abilities are insufficient to achieve perfection. Dr. Paul E. Adolph explains the malady of perfectionism this way: "An attitude that represents dissatisfaction with any achievement or person that is short of perfection, regardless of how fitted or ill-fitted he is to attain to it."[5]

In eternity a perfectionist attitude will result in no true fruit or reward, because those works we do for the glory of ourselves, in our own ability, will be burned up as wood, hay, and straw.

Here is a checklist to help you discover if you are a perfectionist:

1. Are you extremely critical?

2. Are you the type of person who cannot sit down at night until every piece of misplaced clutter is put up into its exact place?

3. Do you apologize when someone comes to your house and the house is not really messed up—you just have not dusted that day?

4. Do you begin jobs that you are not capable of handling and then get frustrated?

5. When you cannot complete a task satisfactorily, are you always trying to find an excuse or blaming someone else for your failure?

6. Do you expect spiritual perfection in others and yourself?

Divine Decontaminant—The Strength of the Spirit

Only God's Spirit can counteract perfectionism (see Psalm 18:32). We must stop trying and start trusting. We must stop playing God in our own lives and in the lives of others. I finally realized that the perfect minister's wife (and the perfect anybody's wife) should discover who she is and identify her talents and spiritual gifts. She should then trust God to help her be the best model of whatever He has chosen for her. Trying to measure up to the impossible dream will only bring frustration.

Don't forget that God majors in things that seem impossible. When I have dared to trust Him, He has enabled me to do things that I know are beyond my natural capacities. The only prerequisite is that I do these things in the power and the strength of the Holy Spirit. Nineteenth-century Swiss theologian Frèdèric Louis Godet said, "Man is a vessel destined to receive God; a vessel which must be enlarged as it is filled and filled in proportion as it is enlarged."

How can we know the difference between serving in our strength and serving in God's strength? There is a key: No frustration or tension results when serving in the strength of the Spirit. So let's say with the Psalmist, "I will go in the strength of the Lord GOD" (Psalm 71:16).

Spiritual Contaminant—The Bondage of Bitterness

If you harbor a grudge in your heart, be it ever so small, it will begin to control you. You will eventually be caught in the bondage of bitterness. The longer you keep your grudge, the more difficult it will be to get free. Bitterness sends down a complex root system that entangles you and chokes out your spiritual life. Hebrews 12:15 contains this caution: "Looking carefully . . . lest any root of bitterness springing up cause trouble, and by this many become defiled." Be assured that bitterness will only bring forth weeds. Leave vengeance to God. Don't steal what belongs to Him. "'Vengeance is Mine, I will repay,' says the Lord" (Rom. 12:19).

Most bitterness comes from simple misunderstanding of supposed wrongs. Some bitterness is the result of genuine wrongdoing on the part of someone else. Even if you have been genuinely wronged, only emotional harm can come to you if you harbor resentment instead of offering forgiveness.

Divine Decontaminant—The Love of the Spirit

The love of the Spirit is clearly needed to overcome these insidious attitudes. But first you must be willing. You must choose to forgive. Then you must confess your own helplessness. Invite Jesus to take over and forgive through you. When He does, it is truly a miraculous process.

A bitter spirit will infect everyone around you. The beautiful Rose of Sharon will slowly but surely become choked out. In His place will grow wickedness and weeds. You will lose both your capacity to forgive others and your capacity to receive forgiveness from God (see Matt. 6:12).

Spiritual Contaminant—The Irritant of Overcommitment

I had a friend who was suffering from colon trouble, backache, and other problems. The doctor told her she was doing too much. I asked her if she had ever invited Jesus into her life. She said that she had as a little child, but that she had gotten away from Him. She knew that she needed to get right with Him and get back into church. She had no time for God and Christian activities.

A wise woman must get her priorities right. If she doesn't have time for prayer, Bible study, ministry to others, and church, her life is out of balance. She will have to completely rearrange her life, or she will be setting herself up for an emotional letdown.

My friend prayed with me that Jesus would become the center of her life. I trusted the Lord to work out the details in her life, but it was her decision. She had to begin.

You may be one of the many women who indiscriminately accepts every request that comes to you. You work until your body is weary and emotional tension builds up. You think you have been serving God, but your strength is sapped, and your motivation is gone.

Divine Decontaminant—The Leading of the Spirit

A wise woman centers her activities around the will of God. To discover His will, she must be still before Him to hear. Jesus did not heal every sick person, raise every dead person, and eat in everyone's home. Jesus did only what the Father sent Him to do (see John 6:38). When you do only those things He is leading you to do, the result is a restful peace of mind.

There are two little letters right in the middle of the alphabet that provide a woman a solution to her problems. They are NO! If she cannot bring herself to use them, she should ask her husband to help her evaluate her activities. She should then follow his advice, as he is her spiritual leader.

You may be doing too much; you may not be doing enough. Stay close to the Savior to guard against either extreme. Save time to fellowship with Him and save time to study His Word and meditate upon it. If you will listen to Him speak through His Word, you will learn to discern His guiding hand in every circumstance.

Spiritual Contaminant—The Dirt of Discontent

Failure to rejoice in the Lord will result in discontentment. We will resent the circumstances in which the Lord has placed us. We may either feel incapable of dealing with our own "opportunities," or we may be envious of the opportunities others have. We may covet the possessions and attainments of others and complain at our own sorrow, sickness, and setbacks.

If we would only realize that the Holy Spirit gives to each woman the gifts that He wants her to have. "But now God has set the members, each one of them, in the body just as He pleased" (1 Cor. 12:18). We shouldn't be discouraged by the giftedness of others.

A spirit of discontentment breeds a critical eye. We become like the man with Limburger cheese on his moustache, who concluded, "The whole world stinks."

Divine Decontaminant—The Sufficiency of the Spirit

It was in a desperate hour of sorrow that God began to reprogram my Christian life. Without time for us even to pray, death reached down into the crib and snatched our little Philip away. I didn't know what to do or what to say. All I could do was hold on to Jesus.

As I was clinging to Him, He reminded me that there was help and comfort in His Word. Through this Book, Jesus began to show me what I should do and what I should say. He pointed me to Psalm 34:1: "I will bless the LORD at all times; His praise shall continually be in my mouth." He showed me 1 Thessalonians 5:18: "In everything give thanks; for this is the will of God in Christ Jesus for you."

I tried to bless the Lord, but I felt like a hypocrite. I did not feel thankful, and I did not feel like praising God. It was then that the Lord showed me that He had not asked me to *feel* thankful but just to obey Him. I discovered that if I could not find and believe my own words, I was free to use His words. I began to give the Lord's words back to Him as an offering of thanksgiving and praise. I did not immediately feel the reality of what I was doing, but I no longer felt like a fake. I knew His words were true.

The more I used His words, the deeper He led me into them. He taught me to say with Job, "The LORD gave, and the LORD has taken away; blessed be the name of the LORD" (Job 1:21). He led me to say with the psalmist, "Because Your lovingkindness is better than life, my lips shall praise You. Thus I will bless You while I live; I will lift up my hands in Your name" (Ps. 63:3-4).

"Better than life, Lord? I thought life was the most priceless possession I could have."

"Better than life, My child!"

These words would cut across my very soul as I offered them to God. Nevertheless, day after day I "faithed" my praise and thanksgiving. He began embedding their reality deep within my heart. I do not know whether it was in the weeks or in the months to follow, but one day I actually *felt* the reality of what I had been saying by faith. Today I can say with my own words and all the reality of my soul, "Thank You, Lord, for the darkest hour of my life. Praise Your holy name!"

My life has not been the same since I discovered this principle: "Not that we are sufficient of ourselves . . . but our sufficiency is from God" (2 Cor. 3:5). The times I have not chosen to practice this principle have been the most frustrating in my life. But when I have chosen by faith to bless the Lord at all times, He has always proven sufficient for every need. From Him I have received peace, power, and growth in my Christian life. I can either try to figure things out on my own, or I can try godly wisdom—looking from God's point of view (see Prov. 3:5-6).

Have you discovered this life-changing principle? If not, begin today. Bless the Lord and give thanks in whatever circumstance you find yourself right now. If this is a joyous time in your life, and you feel like praising— great. If not, don't fake it; faith it. You can use God's Word. Remember that it is true.

*Bless the LORD, O my soul; and all that is within me, bless His holy name!
(Ps. 103:1)*

*Every day I will bless You, And I will praise Your name forever and ever.
(Ps. 145:2)*

*O God, my heart is steadfast; I will sing and give praise, even with my glory.
(Ps. 108:1)*

*I will praise the name of God with a song, and will magnify Him with thanks-
giving. (Ps. 69:30)*

3

The Source of Wisdom

Christ, in whom are hidden all the treasures of wisdom and knowledge.

COLOSSIANS 2:2B-3

My college major was religion. I learned a lot of facts about the Bible, but the emphasis was mainly historical. Through this study, I gained a skeleton of facts, and yet these facts seemed largely dead, irrelevant, distant from my life.

Then a great need in my life caused me to go deeper into the Scriptures. This new approach transformed my study of the Bible. It was so simple I can't imagine how I missed it before. All it involved was looking for Jesus in every book of the Bible that I studied—whether in the Old or the New Testament.

I became excited. Some of the precious treasures were lying right on the surface, while others were hidden in rocky crevices. Some were in the center of a giant mountain that had to be possessed before the treasures could be uncovered. I determined that all the wealth would be mine.

This treasure is Jesus Himself. He is the treasure throughout God's Book. We must constantly search there to find out who He is and what He is like.

JESUS ONLY
Once it was the blessing,
Now it is the Lord;
Once it was the feeling,
Now it is His Word.

Once His gifts I wanted,
Now Himself alone;
Once I sought for healing,
Now the healer own.

Once 'twas painful trying,
Now 'tis perfect trust;
Once a half salvation,
Now the uttermost.
Once 'twas ceaseless holding,
Now He holds me fast.
Once 'twas constant drifting,
Now my anchor's cast.

Once 'twas busy planning,
Now 'tis trustful prayer.
Once 'twas anxious caring,
Now He has the care;
Once 'twas what I wanted,
Now what Jesus says;
Once 'twas constant asking,
Now 'tis ceaseless praise.

Once it was my working,
His it hence shall be;
Once I tried to use Him,
Now He uses me;
Once the power I wanted,
Now the mighty One;
Once I worked for glory,
Now His will alone.[1]

A. B. SIMPSON

BURIED TREASURE

Old Testament Discoveries

I began to search for Him in a seemingly unlikely place—the Old Testament. There I was surprised to see Him from every angle. I saw Him as my Passover Lamb and as my Tabernacle. I saw Him pictured in the lives of Joseph and Isaac. He was everywhere, in every story.

Yes, I have my favorite portraits, and there are some that bless me more than others, but what I can't see through my limited vision might be the one drawn for you. The pictures that seem stern one day might become animated and joyful at the time I need them the most.

The Gospels—Four Views of the Savior

It was a combination of a trip to the Holy Land and my own curiosity that set me on a serious trek into the heart of the four Gospels.

Why are there four of them? Each Gospel contains a different pose of Jesus. I saw Him in Matthew as the King of the Jews, in Mark as the Suffering Servant, in Luke as the Son of Man, and in John as the Son of God. I studied for nine months in these wonderful books. How could I ever have become bored with these divinely inspired Gospels?

Of all the portraits of Christ, my favorite is that of Him as my Passover Lamb. This portrait is like a tapestry with threads from the Old and New Testaments masterfully interwoven. This Lamb was silent before His shearers. How could He have allowed vile men to rail at Him and spit on Him and yet answer not a word? How can I explain what this picture has meant in my life and how much I love Him for remaining silent?

NEVER A WORD

Jesus stood before Pilate;
His accusers stood nearby.
They agreed together to tell
many things that were not so.
But He answered nothing!

Pilate asked, "Why don't You answer;
Don't You hear all the things
they're saying?"
Pilate marveled that
still Jesus answered nothing!

The soldiers then took Jesus
to the judgment hall.
They stripped Him
and robed Him.
They pressed a crown
of thorns into His brow.
They mocked Him and
spat on Him—
hailed Him as

"King of the Jews."
They reviled Him, but
He reviled not!

He was brought as a lamb
to the slaughter—
Spotless and perfect Lamb of God.
But as a sheep who protests
not before her shearers,
so this Lamb opened not
His mouth!

Pilate marveled greatly that
He answered not a word!
I, too, can only marvel at this
Godlike kind of love.

How unlike the Savior I
seem to always be—
With many words I protest and
claim my innocence.

"Oh, make me into Thy likeness!"

I will never comprehend the
Savior's love for me
that never a word came in defense.
He could not explain;
They could not understand—
Though sinless,
He was guilty!

My sins were upon Him:
I deserved the mocking,
the scourging,
the awful pain,
but He bore it all
and answered
never a word!

LOVING JESUS

Inside the life-changing book *We Would See Jesus*, by Roy and Revel Hession, I found the following poem, which has helped to revolutionize my life:

MY GOAL

My goal is God Himself—
Not joy, nor peace,
Nor even blessing—
But Himself, my God![2]

I adopted these words for my goal. I copied them in the flyleaf of my Bible. But more than that, I etched them on my heart. That was many years ago, and the goal of my life has never changed. My lifelong adventure of getting to know and love Jesus has been entirely satisfying. As the Hessions say: "It is enough to see Jesus and to go on seeing Him."[3]

The marriage relationship is an illustration of this spiritual truth. When you enter the door of matrimony, your mate is in the center of your focus. Consciously and unconsciously, he is in your mind and heart at all times. But gradually your aim changes. You discover it is not all moonlight and roses. There are meals to be cooked, floors to be swept, dishes to be washed, and laundry to be done.

Maybe a baby enters your life. The baby has to be fed and cared for. Then another baby arrives and perhaps another after that. The workload increases. You have little time for your "beloved." It wasn't intentional, but your husband becomes just one of the many things in your life. One day you realize your husband is in last place.

You didn't arrive at the marriage altar because you loved to wash dishes and sweep floors. You arrived there for the same reason I did—because you loved your husband so much that you couldn't stand to be apart. All these incidentals held some joy when he was at the center of your relationship.

It is the same with the church's spiritual husband—Jesus Christ. He can't be just one factor in your life. He must be the central factor, your first and only love.

WE NEED TO SEE JESUS

How can we see Him? It's simple really. But it requires consistent effort on our part and enlightening from the Spirit of God. Andrew Murray said, "The love of Jesus must be in the inner chamber, in all my work, in my daily life."[4] In his book *Abide in Christ* he exhorts, "Believer, would you abide in Christ, let it be day by day. A day, just one day only, but still a day, given to abide and grow up in Jesus Christ. In it I may, I must, become more closely united to Jesus."[5]

Here are just a few keys to seeing and knowing Jesus.

Look for Jesus on every page of His Word. You can be sure you will find Him there—from Genesis to Revelation.

Ask the Spirit of God to reveal Jesus through His Word. It is His job to do this (John 16:13-14). We can memorize the words and tell others what Jesus is like, but until our spirits are vitalized by God's Spirit, we never can be enlightened.

Commit yourself to do God's will. Why should God reveal His Son to us if we don't intend to do His will? Our wills should choose to do His will.

Ask for God's power to achieve this knowledge. We can't know Jesus in our own power. But He can give us the power if we will trust Him to do so. Major Ian Thomas says we should say to God: "I can't: You never said I could; You can: You always said You would."[6]

Look for Jesus every day and all day in every circumstance of life. Develop the habit of looking for Him at all times. An intriguing book that can spur you to this habit is *Practicing the Presence of God,* which relates how a seventeenth-century Carmelite monk, Brother Lawrence, made it a habit to communicate with God in every duty, however menial.

IN PRAISE OF JESUS

Can't you hear the voice of wisdom? (Prov. 8:1 TLB)

I believe it is Jesus who calls to us from the book of Proverbs. He invites us to follow Him and find riches and satisfaction through Him, the personification of wisdom. Read and see if you don't think the same thing. Substitute the name of Jesus wherever you find the word *wisdom.*

> *Can't you hear the voice of wisdom [Jesus]? [He] is standing at the city gates and at every fork in the road, and at the door of every house. Listen to what [He] says: "Listen, men!" [He] calls. "How foolish and naive you are! Let me give you understanding. O foolish ones, let me show you common sense! Listen to me! For I have important information for you. Everything I say is right and true, for I hate lies and every kind of deception. My advice is wholesome and good. There is nothing of evil in it. My words are plain and clear to anyone with half a mind—if it is only open! My instruction is far more valuable than silver or gold.*
> *For the value of wisdom [Jesus] is far above rubies; nothing can be compared*

with it [Him]. Wisdom [Jesus] and good judgment live together, for wisdom [Jesus] knows where to discover knowledge and understanding. If anyone respects and fears God, he will hate corruption and deceit of every kind.

Listen to my counsel—oh, don't refuse it—and be wise. Happy is the man who is so anxious to be with me that he watches for me daily at my gates, or waits for me outside my home! For whoever finds me finds life and wins approval from the Lord. But the one who misses me has injured himself irreparably. Those who refuse me, show that they love death. (Prov. 8:1-13, 33-36 TLB)

Proverbs 8:11 declares that "wisdom is better than rubies." Likewise Proverbs 31:10 declares that the price of a virtuous woman is far above rubies. This priceless "wise" woman is filled with Jesus Christ. The New Testament reveals that in Him "are hidden all the treasures of wisdom and knowledge" (Col. 2:3). First Corinthians 1:24 calls Christ "the wisdom of God."

Socrates stated, "The Delphic oracle said I was the wisest of all the Greeks. It is because that I alone, of all the Greeks, know that I know nothing." Socrates, who was wise according to the fashion of this world, thus admitted to being ignorant. And so he was, for true wisdom is to know that we are nothing while God is everything.

God made foolish the wisdom of this world. If we are to be wise, we must turn our eyes from the logic of this so-called liberated age and look only to Jesus.

WOMAN OF THE WORD

A wise woman is filled with the *living* and the *written* Word of God. I want to know and love Jesus, the *living* Word. His *written* Word will point me to Him. The living Word and written Word are inseparable. United in your life, they are the solid rock on which the house of your life can stand.

God's Word is the basis for a woman's authority. If she submits her life to this authority, she will have a sure foundation for her life. God's instructions are given in His Word. If it were not for God's written Word, we would not know what He wants us to be and do.

What kind of book is the Bible? It is a *precious* book. There are many similes for this most priceless book.

YOUR PRECIOUS WORD
Your Word is like a lamp.
It guides me when I
cannot see my way.

Your Word is like a seed.
It must be planted in my life
so it can grow.

Your Word is like a sword
It divides between my judgment
and the wisdom that
comes from You.

Your Word is like a mirror,
Showing me what I'm
really like inside.

Your Word is like milk,
Giving me daily sustenance
that I might live.

Your Word is sweeter than honey.
It's the only remedy when
my spirit turns sour.

Your Word is more precious than gold.
This world's goods cannot compare
with its worth.

I do not doubt Your Word,
for it is settled forever
in heaven (Ps. 119:89).

I love Your Word, so I
think on it all
through the day (Ps. 119:97).

I prize Your Word, for it
teaches me to love right
and hate wrong (Ps. 119:128).

I hope in Your word,
for it is steadfast
and pure (Ps. 119:140).

I rejoice at Your Word, for
it is a precious treasure (Ps. 119:162).

Your commandments are faithful (Ps. 119:86).
Your judgments are right (Ps. 119:75).
Your testimonies are everlasting (Ps. 119:144).

When I am sad, Your Word brings me comfort.
When I am in danger, it gives me hope.
When I am sick, it soothes my brow.
When I am lost, it brings me home.

I will meditate in Your precepts (Ps. 119:78).
I will love Your law (Ps. 119:97).
I will delight in Your statutes (Ps. 119:16).
I will remember Your judgments (Ps. 119:52).
I will believe Your commandments (Ps. 119:66).
I will keep Your Word, for it is my delight.

I am Your servant.
I will not forget Your law.

There is no easy, lazy way to learn God's Word. Study must be daily and consistent. A little knowledge can make us guilty of faulty interpretation. Anyone with fair intelligence can learn facts, but only the "anointing" of the Holy Spirit can teach us truth as we meditate and pray over God's Word. The Bible is full of examples of women who listened when God spoke and obeyed what they heard. God did marvelous works in the lives of these women.

But Satan has always been trying to cast doubt on God's Word. From the beginning he developed the strategy of mixing partial truth and partial error. God said to Adam, "You may freely eat of every tree in the garden except the tree of the knowledge of good and evil." One day Satan came to Eve and subtly inquired, "Has God said you shouldn't eat of every tree of the garden?" (Gen. 3:1, author's translation). Then he told the woman a lie about God: "If you eat of that tree, you will not surely die."

God had provided all that Eve's heart could ever desire. He created her with a prized position as a helper suitable for Adam. He met her every need and placed her in paradise. However, Eve wasn't satisfied. One day she was attracted to a colorful personality who was waiting for the proper time to beguile her. The essence of the first woman's sin was that she didn't believe God's Word. She listened instead to the voice of the serpent.

Modern woman hasn't really changed. Many are still listening to Satan's subtle slanders against God's Word. Satan is still asking, "Has God said?"

Has God said, "I want you to be a helper?" (see Gen. 2:18). You know you're just as smart as any man. You can be the leader!

Has God said, "Be a keeper at home?" It's too boring just being a house-wife. Going into the office, the police force, or the theater is better. That's where the real action is!

Has God said, "Be obedient to your own husbands?" (see Titus 2:5). You don't have to be submissive to anyone but God. You've been liberated!

Has God said, "I do not want you to have a place of teaching and authority over the man?" (see 1 Tim. 2:12). You're a much more gifted communicator than he. You could make the issues much clearer!

Has God said, "The fruit of the womb is a reward?" (see Ps. 127:3). Why, you could ruin your figure. Anyway, children bring such heartache!

God has said many things. Sometimes we aren't listening to hear what He has to say. Other times we hear the message loud and clear, but we rationalize and say that it doesn't apply to us today. He couldn't possibly mean that. Those concepts are so out of date.

God said a crazy thing to a young, unmarried girl named Mary. He told her she was going to have a baby. Besides that, He said she was still going to be a virgin when she was pregnant. Everybody knows that is impossible. Yet this young virgin who heard the word of God, unbelievable as it was, by faith replied, "Behold the maidservant of the Lord! Let it be to me accord-ing to Your word" (Luke 1:38).

God's spoken word was then taken by His Spirit and was formed in the womb of a young woman who believed God. She must have had her fears, her frustrations, and many lonely days of misunderstanding by her friends and family. I doubt that they believed she had received "a word from God." Yet for Mary, the one who listened to God's word, the one who received God's word, to her was given the highest privilege ever bestowed upon a woman. At God's appointed time she brought forth the living Word of God.

But Mary kept all these things, and pondered them in her heart. (Luke 2:19)

> *Oh, to know the heart of Mary—*
> *what a treasure*
> *would be found.*
> *But if I receive His Word*
> *to me, all heavenly blessings*
> *will in me abound!*

4

God's Intention for Women

*And the LORD God said, "It is not good that man should be
alone; I will make him a helper comparable to him." Then the
rib which the LORD God had taken from man He made into a
woman, and He brought her to the man. And Adam said:
"This is now bone of my bones and flesh of my flesh."*

GENESIS 2:18, 22-23

The first woman was created to be an encourager, a motivator. She was a
perfectly suited partner to her husband. I can imagine her saying, "Adam,
the names you picked for the animals are splendid." Or, "Let me help
you, Adam! Being here with you is wonderful!" Adam's eyes must have
brightened as he was inspired on to another job in God's beautiful garden. He loved Eve and appreciated everything she was and did. It was a
perfect relationship.

But then one day the serpent came into the garden. Eve didn't even
bother to ask Adam's advice. She thought she remembered what God had
said, but she must have been daydreaming, because she fell for the serpent's
line. Sin entered the world as Satan's trickery, and lying achieved his desired
purpose.

Part of Eve's punishment was to have her husband "lord it over her."
Perhaps she then felt oppressed and misused. Perhaps she wanted to share
more in his accomplishments. Perhaps he didn't ask for her advice because
he had already seen her poor judgment. No doubt she began to nag and feel

sorry for herself. Perhaps he began to feel unmotivated; the sky wasn't the limit anymore. Now it was just weeds and thorns and hard work.

Years later Solomon was looking for someone who sought after wisdom, as we read in the first chapter of our study together. He had probably looked high and low for just the right woman who would inspire him to fulfill his potential. He observed hundreds of them with no success. He said, "And I find more bitter than death the woman whose heart is snares and nets, whose hands are fetters. He who pleases God shall escape from her, but the sinner shall be trapped by her" (Eccl. 7:26).

As the years passed, some women began to use the same means as Satan to get their own way—deceit and trickery. Since they didn't possess the strength of a man, many times women resorted to deception. Jezebel was such a woman. She sank about as low as a woman can. She misused the office of queen to possess Naboth's vineyard. She wrote letters in her husband Ahab's name and sealed them with the royal seal. She arranged for two false witnesses to testify against Naboth, resulting in his murder. God's judgment against Jezebel was not immediate, but it was sure. She was a woman whose heart was "snares and nets."

IN NEED OF ENCOURAGEMENT

In contrast to this deceitful woman, God can equip you and me to regain our original role as encourager and motivator to our husbands. And there are times when this encouragement can make all the difference in the world.

There was a time when our denomination was in a battle for the integrity of the Bible. Many friends were encouraging my husband to allow his name to be presented as a candidate for the presidency of the Southern Baptist Convention. This office would have a powerful impact on key appointments that could transform the denomination.

Adrian and I prayed about this decision and discussed it together. One concern was that it might be a diversion from his gifting and main calling as a pastor and evangelist. As we discussed the subject, I'd often ask him, "Adrian, on a scale of one to ten, where are you?" Hardly ever was the answer higher than a six.

The evening before the convention, two good friends came by our room to talk to him and to pray about this decision. While they were on their faces before God on the floor of the hotel room, I put on a housecoat and slipped into bed. As they prayed, I also prayed. It seemed that God spoke to my heart clearly. When Adrian lifted his face and looked in my direction, I held up ten fingers.

Later he said this was the confirmation and encouragement that urged him in his decision and proved to be the will of God for his life and our denomination.

There have been countless other less momentous opportunities for me to exhibit these same qualities to build my husband up. In fact, Adrian has commented on how much the nuggets of truth and promises of strength that I find in my quiet time with the Lord and later share with him have encouraged him for "the battle."

CREATIVITY VERSUS DECEPTION

But there is a danger even in this high calling of encouragement. Sometimes it calls us to be creative, but it never calls us to be deceptive. Sometimes even Christian women don't recognize the difference between the two. The godly woman would not want to use deception. Sometimes, however, a woman will manipulate others into doing what she considers many "good" projects. She can't bring herself to trust God to work in the lives of others. Her clever ways are ever before her. Since she considers herself righteous, only God Himself can show this woman her heart of "snares and nets."

In the Bible Rebekah illustrates such a woman. She played favorites between her sons. By trickery she went about to accomplish a good thing. Esau, the eldest, despised his birthright, which afforded him the right of spiritual leadership. Jacob, her favorite, was interested in spiritual things.

She conceived the scheme to have Jacob, who was a smooth man, imitate his brother Esau, who was a hairy man, to deceive Isaac, their blind father. She put goatskins on Jacob's hands and neck so that Isaac would mistake Jacob for Esau and give to Jacob Esau's birthright (see Gen. 27:16). She probably rationalized that the end would justify the means. She accomplished what she set out to do, but much heartache was the result (for herself, her sons, and later for their wives and children)—all because she was a manipulator.

MOTIVATION VERSUS MANIPULATION

God has endowed the woman with the unique role of motivator. Her husband is called on to be the main decision maker. But she can inspire him to greatness. She can motivate him more than any other person through her love and admiration.

There is a fine line between motivation and manipulation. Other people may not always be able to discern the difference. The outward acts may be the same—admiring others and doing thoughtful things, but the woman who is a manipulator is doing these things to get her way. She thinks her way is always best.

Instead, the Holy Spirit inwardly motivates the Christian woman to do good works. He provides the inner spark that can be fanned into a flame. She influences by providing her husband with a positive support, a kind word, a gentle encouragement. How wonderful that God uses human beings as instruments of His motivational power.

I have experienced this temptation in my own marriage. A number of years ago I became convinced that I should adopt a more nutritious way of eating. My husband and children were not as excited or committed to this as I was. I read a book titled *The Sneaky Organic Cook*. It detailed ways to add nutritious ingredients to enrich food—while maintaining good flavor. But my husband began to detect the different tastes, and he discovered that I had added these healthy ingredients. He thought this was manipulative.

Now I have learned that if I want to use a substitute or add a healthy ingredient, I tell him. For instance, in the recipes that had called for ground beef, I began to use either very lean beef or ground turkey, to cut down on our animal fat intake. Then I began to substitute soy hamburger for the meat. But first I told Adrian and asked whether he wanted me to use these substitutes. He responds much better to this, and he considers this a motivation to improve his eating habits rather than manipulation.

If a woman is not controlled by the Holy Spirit, she will probably resort to manipulation. She may subconsciously try to imitate the supernatural force of the Holy Spirit. However, no woman can duplicate His work. How foolish she is to try. The end of manipulation is empty and unfulfilling.

When we invite Christ to control our lives, we will become God's inspiring motivators—in every arena of life—at home, at church, in every relationship. We must ask Him to cleanse our motives and put His glory at the forefront. And He will faithfully begin changing us into the pure vessels He can use to minister to our husbands, our children, our community, and His body.

5

Battle of Identity

Who can find a virtuous wife?
For her worth is far above rubies.

PROVERBS 31:10

The feminist movement makes much of the identity question. There are many side issues, but "Who am I?" seems to be the central factor in the battle for equal rights. The Christian woman must look at the issue from a different perspective.

Without the Word of God as my authority, I too would probably be a proponent of "women's lib." I was encouraged in my youth to excel in subjects that were typically male. I didn't take home economics in high school because it was not considered a worthy subject for those planning to go to college. I was elected president of mixed groups at various times; I tied with another girl for the second highest grades in our graduating class. Even at church I was encouraged to compete with the young men, and I beat two of them (now prominent pastors) in a speakers' tournament.

I don't say this to brag, only to show you that I was a perfect setup for women's lib. It was only the circumstances in my life and the grace of God that kept me from it.

The circumstances that helped counteract my encouragement toward equal authority and leadership roles with men were:

• A happy home where my father was the head, and my mother was submissive.
• A home where I was encouraged in the homemaking arts, where my mother made homemaking her life's work and was fulfilled by it.

- A husband who believed he should be the head of the house.
- A belief in the Bible as the infallible Word of God.

I will be forever grateful for the example of my home and for the leadership of my husband, but if it were not for my belief in the Bible, I could have easily rationalized and dismissed these as being backward and chauvinistic.

So for years I have stood on the Word of God! I have gone back to the Scriptures time and time again to study what they have to say about a woman's place and ministry. I have been tempted many times to take the lead over less capable men, and it has only been God's Word that has kept me from it. Intellectual assent to the Bible, however, does not erase all the problems facing Christian women.

MY JOURNEY

Had it not been for the women's libbers I might not have recognized I had a problem. But as they kept crying, "Identity! Identity!" and kept asking, "Who are you, American woman?" I began to slowly peek out from underneath mountains of diapers. I had given birth to five babies in eight years. My youngest had just started to school, and I hadn't had time to wonder about "who I was" in years.

Christian circles just didn't offer the answers. Sometimes our meetings were so unrelated to real life that Christian women had to turn to the "world" to find the answers. Some women simply work their way through hard times; others accept them as being a part of growing up. I don't know which was my problem; I only know that for the first time I began to ask, "Who am I?"

I began to feel unneeded. I began to reflect on the past when my husband and I had worked for the Lord together. Those desires began to return. I wanted to become involved in his work again. I thought I had tremendous ideas on how to improve everything, but now full-time male staff members were responsible for these details. I began to understand that I was passing through a transitional period of my life. I could not go back to what I had been BC (before children).

If only I had dwelt on "who I have become" instead of "who I used to be." I was not the same person anymore. If I had realized that, I could have escaped some of the resentment that began to form inside of me. I didn't understand myself, and I didn't think anyone else understood me.

A New Me

There was a "me" clamoring to burst forth—a new me. I was similar to that girl of yesterday. You would have recognized many of the same talents and goals, but I had grown into quite a different person than I had been BH (before husband) and BC (before children). The word *grown* is key here.

Would I go back to living in my little rigid world with everything always planned and everything always organized (never having serendipity because of my rigid organization)?

Would I go back to the unbending standard of perfection I had created for myself (that had created tension problems)?

Would I go back to my shallow Christian life with all my pat answers (but no real compassion for those who sinned and sorrowed)?

Would I go back to my self-righteous list of do's and don'ts (always in bondage and always trying to please others instead of God)?

Would I go back to a life of doing things for God (instead of letting God do things through me with Him getting the glory)?

Would I go back to hiding from my inadequacies and fears (instead of facing them in faith and having the true joy of overcoming)?

No, never!

God has used my husband, my children, and the circumstances of life to make me into another Joyce. I used to be happy; now my life is one of rejoicing. I'm thrilled to be Mrs. Adrian Rogers. Others can use Ms. if they want to. I'm happy acknowledging and owning the person I am.

Without Them

I need my husband. When I think something is impossible, Adrian thinks it is possible. Because of his positive spirit I have been overseas numerous times. Because of his positive spirit I have learned I can embark on innovative projects. Throughout our marriage, all the worthwhile things I have done have been done because of the support and encouragement of my husband and children. They have been God's chief tools in pruning me and bringing forth spiritual fruit in my life. Were it not for them, you wouldn't be reading this book.

Without them I would have thought I was adequate, independent, and self-sufficient. I would have tried to do something spectacular with my life to become somebody. Without them I wouldn't have known what true fulfillment as a woman is. I would never have known the fulfillment that love and dependence brings.

Even our little son who was snatched from his crib by death—without him in my life for that little while, I would never have known the comfort of God's Holy Spirit and the inadequacy of my ability to help myself. I wouldn't have learned the priceless lesson of how to comfort those who grieve.

I am proud to be Mrs. Adrian Rogers, wife and mother of four wonderful children. You could never know who I am without knowing these special people God has placed in my life. Jack Taylor said it best: "They [family] are God's perfect gifts to me to help in perfecting me."[1] I am proud to be a part of them, and I am proud that they are a part of me.

MISTAKES AND ABUSES

As long as men and women are in human bodies, we all will be prone to mistakes. Christian men and women are not exceptions to the rule. We just know how to begin again when we make mistakes.

God knew men would make mistakes, sometimes even to the point of abusing their power. How can a woman help to correct these errors without becoming a rebellious nag? She must be filled with the Holy Spirit, thereby manifesting a joyful, thankful heart (see Eph. 5:18-20). She must not neglect her outward appearance, but her primary concern should be on the inner qualities of a meek and quiet spirit. This means she should be both inwardly and outwardly submissive.

She should pray for her husband (and other male leadership), asking God to point out their weak points to them (see Eph. 6:18). She should lovingly entreat her husband in creative ways where she feels it is appropriate. Great wisdom is needed to discern the difference between entreating and nagging (see Prov. 27:15).

She should then trust God to bring pressure to bear on that male authority in her life, expecting God and not the man to work a miracle (see Heb. 13:18). Obedience at each of the preceding levels makes it possible to believe God for the results.

IT FITS ME TO A "T"

Something within me cries out against being a "rubber-stamped copy." With the songwriter I say, "I gotta be me." But as a Christian I have to modify that to say, "I gotta be me—in Christ." I can never find fulfillment in doing simply as I please. My self-centered actions must be surrendered to Christ.

I began my Christian life with the discovery that Christ died for my sins (see Rom. 5:8). It wasn't until later that I became aware of the fact that I was "crucified with Christ" (Gal. 2:20). My old sinful self died that day two thousand years ago. I can count on that fact. My focus now should be on living unto God. "I have been crucified with Christ; it is no longer I who live, but Christ lives in me" (Gal. 2:20).

I am no longer the person I used to be. I am a new creature. I must discover that new person and yield to God. As hard as it may be to see, God is fashioning a masterpiece out of my life.

HIS MASTERPIECE

God said of me, His child,
"You are My workmanship,
My poem, My masterpiece."
Not that I gave outward evidence
of such prospect,
but God saw in me a destiny.

I was like a stone in the heap,
broken and useless,
but God passed by.

He saw me lying there in the dust.
He stopped to pick me up.
He held me in His hand.
By His grace that day,
He brushed away the dust
and began His masterpiece.

In understanding that unique "new me," I must consider at least six areas:

- Temperament
- Training
- Talents
- Treasures
- Tasks
- Time

Temperament

According to Tim LaHaye, there are four basic temperaments. They are discussed at length in his book *The Spirit-Controlled Temperament*.[2] The sanguine and the choleric temperaments are more outgoing, while the melancholy and the phlegmatic temperaments are more introverted.

The sanguine is the bubbly, energetic "life of the party." The choleric is the dominant, aggressive leader. The melancholy is gifted, sensitive, and sometimes moody. And the phlegmatic is the one who always seems to be calm, cool, and collected. Each person has one dominant temperament rounded out and complimented by a combination of the other three.

Each temperament has both strengths and weaknesses. For every strength I need to realize that without Christ I can do nothing (see John 15:5). But the exciting discovery is that the Holy Spirit has strength for every weakness. "I can do all things through Christ who strengthens me" (Phil. 4:13). God designed me in a special way in order for me to meet special needs. No one else can fill my shoes.

Training

Next I need to take a look at my background.

- What kind of family did I come from?
  - Formal or informal
  - Christian or non-Christian
  - Loving or cold
- What type of education did I receive?
  - High school
  - College
  - Graduate school
- What kind of experiences have I had?
  - Traveled or stayed at home
  - Sports-minded or studious
  - Lived in the country or the city

I'm not responsible for some of these factors. God placed me in a particular family with certain financial advantages or disadvantages. I was raised either in a small town or a big city. It wasn't until I grew older that I was able to make choices for myself. I should not, however, despise any of my background experiences, for God has put them in my life to enable me to minister more effectively to others.

Talents

In my "positive probe" I must examine carefully my God-given talents:

- Ability to create art
- Ability to perform musically
- Ability to speak
- Ability to write
- Ability to teach
- Ability to care for children
- Ability to sew
- Ability to cook
- Ability to listen

The sooner I discover my talents, the sooner I can develop them. God will not miraculously supply me with the abilities that I must gain through practice and hard work. I must make an effort to receive training.

If you are a multitalented person, ask the Lord to help you choose which talents to develop to their fullest. Otherwise you will become a "Jill-of-all-trades and master of none." Many "gifted" persons are living frustrated lives because of their own indecision and lack of direction.

Find one talent that you would like to have as your focal point. Let the other talents become a beautiful backdrop across your life. They will add richness and diversity. Perhaps in later years you will find time to develop them.

Treasures

In addition to a Christian woman's natural talents, she also possesses supernatural gifts. They are spiritual treasures to be discovered. God gives each Christian at least one spiritual gift. The various gifts are described in 1 Corinthians 12 and 14 and Romans 12. We should pray and ask the Lord to reveal to us what our gift or gifts are.

Once discovered, the gift should be developed to its highest potential. We can grow in our gifts by being continually filled with the Holy Spirit and by receiving training in areas of ministry where we can effectively use our gifts.

I believe God matches these spiritual treasures to our natural talents and temperaments. For instance, a person with the talent for singing may have the gift of exhortation. If so, she then has a supernatural ability to comfort and build others up in the faith through her singing. Someone else with the gift of mercy might express that gift through the talent of caring for children. A woman with the gift of prophecy could exercise her gift through the talent of writing.

There are endless combinations of talents and gifts. You are a unique individual through whom God wishes to minister to a needy world.

Tasks

I need to remember that my role as a woman is constantly changing. In my lifetime I may wear several different "hats"—wife, mother, grandmother, teacher, pastor's wife. Your hats may be different, depending upon whether God calls you to marry and to be a mother. The death of a mate also changes a woman's task.

As my children matured, my tasks were always changing. As I transitioned from mother to mother-in-law to grandmother, I found many more adjustments in order. Nonetheless, my joyful acceptance of whatever the task I face from year to year is one of the secrets of fulfillment.

Time of Life

The time of life I am in is closely related to my tasks. Jill Renich lists these phases as:

- Childhood
- Learning (educational)
- Childbearing years
- Ministry (after forty)

Renich says, "The latter phase, ministry after forty, can be the peak of a woman's life. She's conquered the learning/mistakes era and is able to forge ahead with the wisdom acquired in earlier years. She maintains the vitality of the middle years, but adds to it the maturity, mellowness, and wisdom of the older years."

As I progress from one phase of my life to another, my life changes. It is enlarged by the circumstances that have surrounded it. Just as teenagers experience some growing pains when they come through adolescence, so I can expect to experience the same things when I go through transitional years.

We may need to spend some extra time to gain understanding of our place in life when we realize that all our children have grown up. We may have to rediscover who we really are. On the other hand, if you have no children, you may need something extra to fill the void in your life and provide you with fulfillment.

By nature a woman is more emotional than a man. We must take care of ourselves physically and spiritually to make it through these phases of our lives. But most of all, we must lean on the Lord for our emotional stability as we pass through each phase of life and appreciate its unique joys.

PART TWO

Wisely Under Authority

6

God's Authority

*Let every soul be subject to the governing authorities.
For there is no authority except from God, and the authorities
that exist are appointed by God.*

ROMANS 13:1

Some years ago we experienced an earth tremor in Memphis, Tennessee. I will never forget it. I was sitting in church when the chandelier overhead began to sway slightly. One person, then another, began slowly to get up before anyone really grasped what was happening. I finally reached my family, and we were grateful that by that time the tremor was over. On the way home my youngest daughter, Janice, asked, "Mama, what do you do when there is an earthquake?" Besides a few practical suggestions, I answered, "Remember, Janice, God is in control." Yes, He is sovereign. He is over all.

That evening when we arrived home, I got my Bible and reread a passage of Scripture I had read in my morning devotions that had puzzled me. Psalm 18:10 said, "And He rode upon a cherub, and flew; He flew upon the wings of the wind." God was symbolically pictured as flying upon a cherub. As I meditated on this verse in the light of the evening's happenings, I concluded that this verse was saying that God is in control; He is not in a panic. He sees the storms, the earthquakes of life, and they are under His feet. The psalmist tells us in verse sixteen, "He sent from above, He took me, He drew me out of many waters."

I can put my confidence in a God who is in control not only of the literal floods and earthquakes, but also of the tremors in my life. I can also trust Him that at His appointed time He will rescue me so that the circumstances of life will be under my feet.

The psalmist said, "You have put all things under His feet" (Ps. 8:6). God indeed established a line of authority, and He is the main authority over all things. This is not an oppressive thought, but rather the most comforting concept in my life—God is in control. He is over all, and He is in charge.

GOD'S LINE OF AUTHORITY

Though equality exists in the Godhead, there is a spiritual line of authority. God the Father is the head of God the Son (see 1 Cor. 11:3). This does not indicate inferiority. God the Father has chosen to give His Son the highest place of honor. "Every knee should bow, and that every tongue should confess that Jesus Christ is Lord, to the glory of God the Father" (Phil. 2:10-11).

God has committed all judgment to the Son. This Son, who humbled Himself and willingly left heaven to die in our place, has received from His Father a name which is above every name (see Phil. 2:9). But 1 Corinthians 15:27-28 declares, "For He has put all things under His feet, then the Son Himself will also be subject to Him who put all things under Him, that God may be all in all."

The Father is the one who put all things under the Son. There was no jealousy in the Godhead—no striving for first place—only different positions. Jesus had been appointed such a place of honor that there was no coveting of position. After all, it was Jesus who not only was sent by the Father to be a servant and to die, but it was Jesus who willingly gave His life for us. They are in such complete oneness that thoughts of competition never occur.

I WAS SENT

I was sent
  by My Father
  into the world.
I must work His works!

I didn't come to do My will;
  He sent Me to do His will.
I didn't come to speak My words;
  He sent Me to speak what
  I heard Him say.

My Father told Me
  to tell you
  to believe in Me,

to love Me,
to honor Me.
If you don't honor Me,
  you don't honor my Father
  who sent Me.

If you believe in Me,
  My Father will give you
  everlasting life;
I will raise you up at
  the last day.

You can have that life right now.

The living Father sent Me,
  And I live by the Father.
If I am your bread, you
  shall live by Me.
True life will begin today,
  and you shall live forever.

So you want to see My Father!
If you've seen Me,
  you've seen Him
  who sent Me.

I and My Father are one, and
  I always do those things
  that please Him.
Soon I'm going back to My Father—
  to Him that sent Me.
That's really best for you
  because when I go,
  I'm going to send another—
  the Comforter, My Spirit!

He'll not only be with you
  as I have been;
He'll be in you.
  He'll never leave you;
He'll glorify Me.
  He'll show you all things.

> *Then you'll really know Me—*
> *The One the Father sent.*
> *Then I'll be in you as the*
> *Father is in Me.*
> *And as the Father has sent Me,*
> *even so will I send you*
> *That others too may know*
> *that I was sent.*

It is difficult for us to comprehend someone being over another without feelings of superiority or someone being under another without feelings of inferiority. But God demonstrated in Himself the concepts of true equality of worth and oneness while maintaining a consistent line of authority.

It is not offensive to God the Son that God the Father is His head (see 1 Cor. 11:3). He never rebelled when His Father sent Him to be the Savior of the world (see John 17:18). He never complained that He only got to do what His Father told Him to do and that He only got to say what His Father told Him to say (see John 8:28-29).

Hebrews 5:8-9 says, "Though He was a Son, yet He learned obedience by the things which He suffered. And having been perfected, He became the author of eternal salvation to all who obey Him." For when Jesus, the Son, was under the authority of His Father, He was then given the authority over heaven and earth (see Matt. 28:18).

If we can only see what God has in store for us, what authority He wants to give us if we can learn to live *under* authority. He said, "Blessed *are* the meek, for they shall inherit the earth" (Matt. 5:5). We can have all things under *our* feet if we are in Christ—living in submission to Him and to those to whom He has delegated authority.

UNDER GOD'S PROTECTION

How precious is Your lovingkindness, O God! Therefore the children of men put their trust under the shadow of Your wings. (Ps. 36:7)

The Bible symbolizes God's protection in various ways. One of my favorites is "under His wings." So when I yield to His authority in my life, I reap the benefits of living "under His wings." The hymn-writer William O. Gushing has beautifully expressed this thought.

Under His wings I am safely abiding;
Tho' the night deepens and tempests are wild,
Still I can trust Him; I know He will keep me;
He has redeemed me, and I am His child.

Under His wings, what a refuge in sorrow!
How the heart yearningly turns to His rest!
Often when earth has no balm for my healing,
There I find comfort, and there I am blest.

Under His wings, O what precious enjoyment!
There will I hide till life's trials are o'er;
Sheltered, protected, no evil can harm me;
Resting in Jesus I'm safe evermore.

Under His wings, under His wings,
Who from His love can sever?
Under His wings my soul shall abide,
Safely abide forever.

In every area of our lives God has delegated various authorities for our protection. In essence through these authorities He is saying, "I love you; don't hurt yourself." We sometimes chafe under this supposed bondage, thinking how wonderful it would be if we could only be free of those over us.

Just suppose that there were no speed limit in a school zone. Many of us might run over a careless child. If there were no parents to tell a child what time to go to bed and what nutritious foods to eat, children would be unhealthy and die at an early age. If there were no pastors to warn of false doctrines, many would be led astray and go to a Christless eternity.

Jesus wept over Jerusalem. He wanted to gather her children together, even as a hen gathers her chickens under her wings (see Matt. 23:37). He longed to protect His people, but they refused. Truly, to come under His delegated authority is to be covered by His protection.

FREEDOM UNDER AUTHORITY

God is the undisputed one in charge of this universe. It would have been no problem for Him to have a corner on all authority and not to share it with anyone. He could have spoken His commands and wishes audibly for all to hear. At a certain time each day He could have all human beings stand at attention to get their daily instructions from their Authority. He could have ruled the universe any way He chose. How marvelous that He chose to share His authority with us. God set up specific spheres of influence for our lives and delegated His authority in these areas. He has done this for our protection. His plan of authority is good and upright, the best for us; only human sin causes the abuses and misuses of His delegated authority among people.

Twenty centuries ago Jesus Christ stepped onto the scene. Prejudice against women had become so bad that a man wouldn't even speak to a woman in public. She wasn't allowed the privilege of an education. She had become a sex object and was considered unworthy to do more than the menial tasks. Yet there were great traces of God's original purpose in women. Man couldn't do without her. He knew he needed her—even if the reason wasn't clear.

When Jesus died, He freed the woman from her bondage. Galatians 3:28 reveals, "There is neither Jew nor Greek, there is neither slave nor free, there is neither male nor female; for you are all one in Christ Jesus." This means that male and female are equal in worth before God. He corrected the abuses that had come through man's sinful nature. He declared that if we wanted to experience the reality of this freedom, we must know Him. Listen to His words:

Therefore if the Son makes you free, you shall be free indeed. (John 8:36)

And you shall know the truth, and the truth shall make you free. (John 8:32)

I am the way, the truth, and the life. (John 14:6)

God's Freedom Demonstration—Jesus Christ

What does this new freedom mean? Are we free to do as we please? Do we even know the true meaning of freedom? Before we attempt to assert our rights for freedom, we would do well to study God's concept of freedom. Our freedom is found in Jesus Christ. Shouldn't we look to Him for guidance? He was God's demonstration of freedom. What did He think freedom meant?

God declared His blueprint for revolution that would bring about freedom in the Gospel of John:

For I have come down from heaven, not to do My own will, but the will of Him who sent Me. (John 6:38)

I do nothing of Myself; but as My Father taught Me, I speak these things. And He who sent Me is with Me. The Father has not left Me alone, for I always do those things that please Him. (John 8:28b-29)

Woman's Freedom Demonstration

Jesus demonstrated His freedom by doing only what the Father told Him—every moment He was on earth. Isn't this the way we as women should demonstrate our freedom?

God's will for women is for us to discover His original intention before sin entered the world. What was the woman's role then? Helper! Partner! Motivator! Modern woman has wanted more than to be freed from the abuses that have resulted from sin. She has wanted to change her God-given role. It is as if she looks up at God and dares to say, "God, I've got a better idea. Let me be the leader half of the time, and let the man be my helper. Then half of the time he can lead, and I'll be the helper. Lord, I'll call it 'egalitarianism.' I think this would be real freedom—real equality."

A Bad Example

There was one long ago who didn't like the role God had given to him, although he was a beautiful creature. He was second in authority to God, but he thought himself far too beautiful and superior to be number two and said, "I will be like the Most High." In making this declaration, Satan became the greatest usurper of authority of all time. And we all know what his eventual end will be.

The Bible says a woman is not to teach or usurp authority over the man (see 1 Tim. 2:12). And yet many women are saying by their actions, "I'm far too beautiful, far too superior to just be a helper for the man. I will change my role. I will be number one. I know more about what is best for me than God."

Only obedience to God's Word brings true freedom. The truly submissive wife finds that her husband and her God release her to a freedom unknown by others.

SUBMIT TO HIM, LORD?

Submit to him, Lord?
  I'm just as smart as he!
Let him be my head?
  You're the only head I need.

My education is lying waste.
  I learned so many things I must
  share to make this world
  a better place.

I'll not be a doormat.
  Help meet his needs?
Who'll help meet mine?
  If I stick with this thing
  called marriage,
  it'll be fifty-fifty or no go!

I have my rights.
  I'm not inferior to any man!
The very least I've earned
  is equal rights!

What's that, Lord?

You stepped down from glory;
  You humbled yourself
  even though You had equal rights
  with God the Father?

You were obedient unto death
  even though You were a King?
You let them spit on You, Lord,
  even curse Your holy name?

The reason why You came was not to
  do Your will, but his?
Because You obeyed, the Father did what?
  He exalted You,
  gave You a name above every name?

Oh, Lord, forgive me!
I never realized.
I thought to submit meant
*   that I was inferior.*

I don't have to gain equality
*   for myself?*

If I obey, You will lift me up?
What, Lord?
If I'm truly submissive,
*   my children will rise up*
*   and call me blessed,*
*   my husband will praise me,*
*   and You, Lord—*
You will honor me?
Then give me a submissive heart,
*   oh Lord.*
I want to be in Your perfect will!

Am I then to become nothing? A "yes" person parroting the wishes and opinions of my husband? "Yes, dear!" "That's right, dear!" "Anything you say, dear!" Who ever got the idea that a woman would lose her identity if she would become a submissive helper? No man wants a doormat—a nothing person with no opinions—no distinctives that make her unique. A woman like that is not a helper but a hindrance. If you were just like him, he would not need you.

If only we could see what God has in store for us, what authority He wants to give us if we learn to live under authority. He said, "Blessed are the meek [the submissive] for they shall inherit the earth" (Matt. 5:5). We can have all things under our feet if we are in Christ—living in submission to Him and to those to whom He has delegated authority.

7

God's Direction

He will choose our inheritance for us . . . .

PSALM 47:4

It may sound easy for me to entreat you to trust God's plan, to submit willingly to His authority, to cheerfully accept His unique will for your life. But, I assure you, I speak to you not from a platform of superiority but from the depths of firsthand experience. Let me describe the big-picture drama God has directed for me. Perhaps then you will understand that I do not glibly tell of God's guidance, but I have walked the path, made good choices and bad, and in the end found God's way the only road to satisfaction.

As a teenager I felt God leading me into a full-time Christian vocation. It later developed that the particular field was to be a minister's wife. I loved all phases of church work, so I knew I would be happy.

Adrian and I were married while still in college, and he was called to a small country church. We were happy there, serving the Lord as we continued our schooling. I taught all the teenagers and helped conduct a Christian recreation program on Saturday evenings.

After three years we moved to the seminary. While there, we were called to another small church. I continued to teach all the teenagers, sing, and do home visitation with my husband.

With schooling behind and three additions to our family, we were called to a somewhat larger church—our first full-time pastorate. Life became involved as different jobs in the church opened, and my family grew even larger. But I was happy despite being busy raising a family and serving the Lord. Our church grew, but was still an average-size church. I felt at home there.

We were then called to a church with fewer in attendance but with a great potential for growth. We knew God had called us there. The Lord began to add more and more to His church in that place.

I began to feel a little apprehension. I had never wanted to go to a big church. I had voiced that preference several times. Outwardly I was able to keep up appearances, but inwardly I was in turmoil. The Lord has since shown me that I was inwardly fearful—fearful of being unneeded, of being outgrown, of not being capable, fearful of being shut out of my husband's time. The more the church grew, the more he was gone.

One day I discovered this wasn't the role I had chosen so willingly. This wasn't the role I loved and was comfortable in. Self-pity crept into my life— even resentment. I became frustrated. At times I would feel a deep loneliness, even when surrounded by hundreds of people. I longed for someone to understand. Pride kept me from admitting to anyone that I was dissatisfied with my role. I felt defeated.

It is as if I said to God, "I didn't choose this plan. I want another version altered to my specifications. I don't believe You can readjust and enlarge my life to fit into Your plan."

It was as if God replied, "You thought you could do something—but not this. You can't do anything without Me."

He taught me some wonderful truths in those days:

The Lord never deals with us alike. That is why we shouldn't be too enamored with someone else's experience.

God is sufficient to deal with my family and friends Himself. So we must let God make the choices (we are, after all, under His authority) and offer our services to Him to use as He sees fit.

When God snatched the rug out from under me through the death of my third baby, I looked up to see Him standing there with His hand outstretched saying, "Get up, my child, and lean hard on Me." And I did! I recognized there was nothing else I could do.

God was using His sure-win method on me. He was bringing me to the end of myself. You can come the long way or take the shortcut—whichever way you choose. But if you are a child of God, you will eventually come to the end of yourself and arrive at the way out of your problem. The way out is Jesus Christ. If only I had believed, He could have made me adequate in the first place. Instead I chose the long, hard way to discover that He is able.

"I can do all things through Christ who strengthens me" (Phil. 4:13). I had memorized those words as a teenager. If anyone knew their meaning,

I thought I did. But did I really? When I finally came to Jesus Christ and stopped trying my own shortcuts, I said to Him, "Lord, I'm totally dependent on You. I didn't choose this way, but You know best. I'm going to believe that You can enlarge my life—make me supernaturally adequate. I'm going to stop saying 'I can't' and say 'You can.'"

I know that works. It was 1970 when I stood at the end of myself and looked into the face of Jesus with nowhere else to go. In the decades that followed, it has been miraculous what He has done in and through my life in areas in which I was, in my own strength, quite inadequate.

In fact, about a year after I allowed the Lord to control my defeated life, a "call" came to go to a really large church. It was the size I had always dreaded. My first reaction was, "Oh no!" I remember saying those very words out loud. Then I could almost feel God's hand on my shoulder as He whispered, "Don't be a fool after all I have shown you in the past year."

That was enough reminder for me. Even before my husband knew for sure, down deep I knew God wanted us to go. The greatest of all miracles was that I was willing to go or stay. The Lord gave me an inner peace that everything was going to be all right. That doesn't mean there was no pain involved in the move. It is hard to move. The only way I can describe it is that it was like an operation. Part of my life was amputated. It was painful.

We lived on an island, and we had to cross a bridge to leave our home of eight years. Things had gone pretty well that last morning in our old home. I had kept busy with packing and cleaning, but when we crossed the bridge, I could almost feel the knife cutting away that part of my life. I couldn't stop the tears. But behind the tears was a willing heart that affirmed: "I'm leaving a part of me back there, Lord. But it's all right. I know You want us to go."

No one said much for several miles. What we all felt inside was too private to talk about at that moment. But after a while the stabbing pain of separation was over. The operation was a success. God gave a sweet assurance of His presence. The lovely memories will always be with me, but a brand-new chapter in my life was beginning.

It's an odd feeling, being "in-between." I didn't know except by faith whether others at our destination would love me like those I had just left. I wondered how the children would adapt. The youngest two, David and Janice, moved with us. The two teenagers, Gayle and Steve, were left behind, one for two months and the other to go to college. Their lives were radically changed because of our move. All this caused doubts. However, I had an inward peace about God's leading. I would commit each difficulty to the Lord as it arose. Only He knew what lay ahead.

I could never have known that day how God would honor that commitment made by faith. The love that waited for me in this huge church was more than I could fathom. For example, since my marriage I have never lived near my mother, and our new church in Memphis, Tennessee, was a thousand miles away from home. This didn't surprise God. He planned it so that there were many "mothers" in that church who patted me and told me they loved me. At first I felt like asking them, "How do you know you love me? You don't even know me yet." But they did love me. They loved me by faith, and they continue to love me.

It was amazing how God orchestrated the transition so that everyone moved in to fill the void created by my recent "operation." I responded to that love. Soon that "loving by faith" became a reality. And once again God's direction proved the only right and best path for our family. I suppose that fact was never in doubt.

8

Some Will Have Husbands

But I want you to know that the head of every man is Christ,
the head of woman is man, and the head of Christ is God.

1 CORINTHIANS 11:3

One sphere of influence where we encounter authority is in the home. The home was instituted by God in the Garden of Eden and takes precedence in its importance and influence over all other areas of life. Although some women (and men) are called to the single life, for most God provides a mate.

God had an orderly plan for marriage and the home. He saw the need for a leader—someone in charge. He placed the man at the head of the home. "But I want you to know that the head of every man is Christ, the head of woman is man, and the head of Christ is God" (1 Cor. 11:3), wrote the apostle Paul. Again he wrote to the church in Ephesus: "Wives, submit to your own husbands, as to the Lord. For the husband is head of the wife, as also Christ is head of the church; and He is the Savior of the body" (Eph. 5:22-23).

This position was in no wise a put-down on the woman to show that she was inferior. In the same verse God demonstrates the submission of Christ to God the Father, and we have already seen this was not demeaning to Christ. Position has nothing to do with these feelings of superiority versus inferiority. Sin has caused the abuses and misuses of our God-given positions. We must learn to deal with sin instead of trying to change roles. If we do change our roles and sin continues, it will only result in worse heartache.

So the man is God's appointed leader in the home. But the woman also has authority in the home. She is over her children along with her husband and under his leadership. Ephesians 6:1 says, "Children, obey your parents." She is also over the management of the home. She is to be a "keeper at home," to guide or rule the affairs of her home (Titus 2:5).

God has delegated His authority in the home to the father and the mother, but Dad has the final word. This does not mean the man should rule excessively or selfishly. That would be an abuse. Although that is sometimes caricatured as a norm for those who believe in male headship, nothing is farther from the truth. The man who leads with a servant spirit wins the loving fellowship of his family.

LOVING FELLOWSHIP AT HOME

One year I bought my husband a little figurine Valentine that said, "Loving you is what I do best." I want this to be one of my greatest achievements. It's so easy to slide into a dull humdrum routine, maintaining a status quo. Yesterday's courtesy and charm won't suffice for today. A love that continues to flourish after marriage is what kept my husband and me together from grammar school to the present time. Our love continues to grow. This growth needs to be balanced in all three areas of our lives—the spiritual, psychological, and physical.

Spiritual Growth

Christ wants us to "grow up into Him" together. Although we may be different in temperament, our basic beliefs and goals must be the same if we are going to grow together. To begin with, we should date and marry someone who is at a similar stage of spiritual growth. Then the partner's earnest desire for the future should be "to be like Jesus."

We should feel comfortable praying with each other, discussing spiritual things, and serving the Lord together. Christian friends and church activities will be some of the means in our spiritual growth. But the home is the chief laboratory for learning. At home we have stripped off our facade, enabling us to recognize more clearly our growth as well as our failures.

Our love will be richer if we are able to share our deepest spiritual desires with our partner. As we grow together in Christ, we will be able to help one another more and more. We will need to learn to temper our "help" with love so our partner will recognize it as help instead of harshness. There is no better guide to what love is all about than 1 Corinthians 13.

Psychological Growth

The second part of this relationship is psychological. The truly smart woman will never pit her intelligence or wit against the man she loves. There are many areas where she can excel without "locking horns" with him. An underlying principle for a successful marriage is "don't compete with your partner—but complete your partner."

The greatest Christian women I know have a gentle reticence when in their husband's presence. They are genuine helpmeets. They are talented and gifted, but they exercise these talents and gifts in a wise way—never in competition with their husbands. Doing this will release your husband to admire and encourage you. Don't, however, carry this to an extreme. We ought never to be so uninformed that we aren't interesting conversation partners. We ought to keep abreast of the major current events.

Learning to communicate effectively our dreams and desires along with our fears and dislikes is a skillful art. We must grow in this ability. To allow someone to see us as we really are is a frightening experience. We long for approval, encouragement, and admiration. Careless and damaging remarks about our partner's inner thoughts can cause a lifetime of wounded feelings. But we can also learn from our mistakes. Forgiveness is the watchword for a successful marriage. For every effort at forgiveness a marriage grows by leaps and bounds.

Physical Growth

There is a unique fulfillment in the sexual realm of marriage. One woman, one man, one flesh was God's idea. Ironically, this sexual fulfillment never precludes acceptance and enjoyment of the unique individuality of the other person. Only then can the physical relationship become a genuine expression of true love and care of the other person.

Sexual enjoyment and loving expressions will increase in meaning and satisfaction as we grow in every area of our marriages. There must be a balance between inner and outer beauty. We must constantly be aware of cleanliness and good grooming. Neglect in these areas will diminish the degree of physical satisfaction. There are, however, many beautiful women who have lost their husbands to someone far less attractive. Nagging, criticism, and a sour, bitter spirit can kill physical enjoyment.

On the other hand, nothing will enhance it more than admiration and encouragement.

Biblical Submission

In his outstanding book *The Christian Family,* Larry Christenson says,

> To be submissive means to yield humble and intelligent obedience to an ordained power or authority. The example God gives is that of the Church being submissive to the rule of Christ. Far from being degrading, this is the Church's glory! God did not give this law of wives being submissive to their husbands because He had a grudge against women: on the contrary, He established this order for the protection of women and the harmony of the home. He means for a woman to be sheltered from many of the encounters of life. Scripture knows nothing of a 50-50 "democratic marriage." God's order is 100-100. The wife is 100 percent a wife, the husband 100 percent a husband.[1]

I, as a Spirit-filled wife, should willingly choose to be submissive to my husband because I know God has ordained this order for my protection and welfare. The husband, of course, carries a great responsibility. He has been appointed by God to be the head of his wife, even as Christ is the head of the Church (see Eph. 5:23). He is to love his wife as Christ loved the Church. This will prevent him from being harsh and dictatorial (see Eph. 5:25). He should set an example of obedience and submission to God and His Word. If his wife and children see him exceeding the speed limit, hedging on the income tax, not returning incorrect change, having a disrespectful attitude toward public officials, or not keeping any of God's commandments, he is tearing down his own authority.

A wife should exhibit before her children an example of obedience to God, her husband, and other authorities. If she runs down her husband to her children, not holding him in high esteem, she is undermining not only his, but her own authority. However, if she lives under authority, God gives her the hearts of her children, and she rules with authority.

I remember a time when my then teenage son Steve had done something wrong (I can't remember what), and I told him to bend over the bed as I administered corporal punishment. I'm still amazed that he did it without resistance. He was stronger than I at the time.

As I look back, I think there were probably several reasons. He had been taught to respect his mother. Also, he knew he had done wrong and had been taught that the Bible encouraged discipline. But he also knew that his dad's authority stood behind me and that if he wasn't submissive to my authority and discipline, he would meet Adrian's authority when he came home, and it would be even harder.

There was mercy at our house for true, undelayed repentance, but there was sure discipline for several things—for being untruthful, disrespectful, and deliberately disobedient. These were seldom exhibited at our house, for the surety and swiftness of discipline had been demonstrated.

When a wife stays under her husband's protective authority, she is shielded physically, emotionally, and spiritually. Paul says in 1 Corinthians 11:10, "Therefore she [the wife] should be subject to his [her husband's] authority and should have a covering on her head as a token, a symbol of her submission to authority, because of the angels" (AMP). When a wife rebels against her husband's authority, she is behaving like Satan and his host of rebels. The Bible says, "Rebellion is as the sin of witchcraft" (1 Sam. 15:23). When a wife rebels against authority, she opens herself to evil influences, to those fallen angels who still live in rebellion against God and are seeking to oppress, obsess, and possess the lives of human beings.

When a woman lives under her husband's authority, she is protected against satanic forces, and she can have power in prayer, she can exercise her spiritual gifts, and she can have authority over Satan and his demons. If we as wives are rebellious, we leave our lives open to Satan. He can use his influence to get through a tiny crack in our spiritual armor and build a stronghold of doubt, fear, exaggeration, pride, lust, laziness, and a multitude of other sins. If we are living under authority, we can resist Satan, and he will flee (see James 4:7). What victory we can know in the spiritual realm!

SOMEONE WHO TRULY HELPS

God created the first helper. "And the LORD God said, 'It is not good that man should be alone; I will make him a helper comparable to him'" (Gen. 2:18). God made Adam and Eve to rule, to have dominion over the earth (see Gen. 1:28). Eve was not meant to be a slave, but she was meant to serve. She was the part of Adam that was missing, and he was thrilled that she was a valuable part of his team.

God didn't spell out exactly what the woman was to do, because it would depend on the situation and the circumstances. Man is not from woman, but woman from man (see 1 Cor. 11:8).

A submissive wife has been caricatured as a doormat type of person—waiting on her husband hand and foot. A helper isn't just a "yes person." *The Saturday Evening Post* had a cartoon that showed an overbearing boss walking down the hall with an obviously new employee. He was saying, "Another thing I can't stand, Snively, is a 'yes man.' Do you understand that?"

We would all like someone to admire us and think our ideas are super. But deep inside we also want someone to be honest with us, point out our weaknesses, and challenge us to live on a higher plane. If someone, whether our mate, our best friend, or our associate, always tells us how wonderful we are and never challenges any idea, we are left with an empty feeling. They are either totally uninformed on the subject we are discussing, or they so fear controversy that they cannot express a contrary opinion.

Either way these people close the door on creativity. There is nothing more uplifting to me than to be in a brainstorming session with one or more persons who challenge my creativity, and together we emerge with an idea much better than I could have thought of on my own.

The secret of being that valuable associate/consultant is sensitivity. First, as wives we should be secure in our position, knowing it is a God-appointed role. That role is the daily supervision of the household and the children.

With this foundation we are ready to be counselors to our husbands. But we must be sensitive to the time when our counsel would be best received. This should be a matter of prayer. When our husbands are tired or have other matters of pressing importance to them, it would be a poor time to bring up a subject contrary to the direction of their present thought.

My husband doesn't like to discuss "heavy" or controversial subjects during fun or recreational times. It's hard for me not to think of subjects that are important to me at those times. For at last I have his undivided attention—or do I? I have discovered that he will resist some topics of discussion at a time for a pleasant walk or a picnic or a ride in the country. He has another agenda—to clear his mind of business-type matters and to relax. He wants me to enter into his present priority. Sometimes a "lighter" subject will suddenly become "heavy," and we as wives should be sensitive enough to know when to "table it" until later.

Queen Esther was a wise woman in this regard. As we will study in depth later, she had a serious matter to discuss with her husband, the king. She was careful to prepare for this important discussion. She wasn't manipulative, but she was wise. She prepared an elegant dinner. She didn't merely "spring" the request on him. She had a plan.

She didn't just prepare dinner, but she prepared herself spiritually. She fasted, and she asked others to fast with her. She focused on God for her help. We should seek God's face and prepare ourselves before we counsel with our husbands, especially on serious matters.

If there is a matter of counsel or correction that we need to discuss, we should be careful to be kind, to say something complimentary before we give the word of correction. Consider how you would feel under similar circumstances. "Let your speech always be with grace, seasoned with salt," reminds the apostle Paul in Colossians 4:6. And remember the proverb that says, "A word fitly spoken is like apples of gold in settings of silver" (Prov. 25:11).

One's heart attitude should be a sincere desire to function successfully in this role of helper. A helper must know the philosophies, goals, and desires of the one in charge. She should be in basic agreement with these overarching goals. If she isn't, she is headed for trouble. That issue should be evaluated and settled before marriage. It is unfortunate when these basic issues are clouded over with the blinders of romance. They will rise to haunt couples after the honeymoon is over.

Of course, there's plenty of room for differences of opinion underneath these overarching goals and philosophies. In the right attitude and timing a wife may express her differences of opinion and make appropriate appeal. Love may demand that we confront our mate on some issues. If a wise woman remains silent when she believes her husband's decisions are unwise, she may carry a deep and sullen rebellion inside that will harm their relationship and ultimately come out and have to be dealt with.

An intelligent, sensitive, creative wife is a tremendous asset to her husband. But there comes a time when a decision must be made. A wife must then yield to her husband's decision. If she thinks that decision is definitely wrong, she then must make her final appeal to heaven's court—to her God in prayer. If it's a matter that disagrees with God's clear commandments, then she must obey God instead of her husband and trust God with the consequences. "We ought to obey God rather than men" (Acts 5:29b). But if it's a matter of taste or judgment in matters that are not of a moral nature, she should sublimate her desires and be supportive of her husband's wishes with God's help.

9

Authority in the Community

Let every soul be subject to the governing authorities.
For there is no authority except from God,
and the authorities that exist
are appointed by God.

ROMANS 13:1

Everywhere you go, you meet authority. You might not recognize it until you need it, but it is there. If it is not, the result is chaos. You may seldom see the manager of a restaurant, but if someone makes a disturbance, he will likely make a quick appearance.

You may decide it is a small thing to run a red light or a stop sign or exceed the speed limit. But if you cause an accident, soon the lights will be flashing and sirens blaring, and "authority" will appear.

A child may constantly be a behavior problem, causing disturbance in the classroom, disrupting the learning process for himself and others. The teacher will exercise her authority through correction or low conduct grades. If this doesn't suffice, the child can be taken to a higher authority, the principal's or counselor's office.

How I praise God for a system of orderly authority. It is built into every area of life—home, government, church, business, school—everywhere. God planned it this way. He means it for our protection and good. He has chosen to involve us in His governing process. He delegated His authority in different spheres of life to different people.

SPIRITUAL AUTHORITY IN THE CHURCH

The New Testament pattern clearly shows that spiritual authority was given to the church. God's plan of delegated authority for the church is that under Christ pastors or elders are "in charge." They watch for our souls. The pastor's authority should not be self-conscious, lording it over others. He should have a servant spirit as his own Lord did. This was best illustrated when Jesus took a towel and washed His disciples' feet. Nonetheless, the pastor will communicate a God-given authority that others recognize and follow. He is the under-shepherd, Jesus being the Chief Shepherd over him.

Consider these Scriptures: "Remember those who rule over you, who have spoken the word of God to you, whose faith follow, considering the outcome of their conduct" (Heb. 13:7). "Obey those who rule over you . . . for they watch out for your souls" (Heb. 13:17a).

Certainly there have been abuses in the role of pastor. The Ghana tragedy some years ago, when Jim Jones led one thousand followers to the supposed "promised land," only to commit mass suicide, is sufficient warning to the gullible. If a pastor is not teaching and living the truth of God's Word, he forfeits his God-given authority.

God has also given deacons to be helpers in the leadership role of the church. The office of deacon is a sacred responsibility with high qualifications (see 1 Tim. 3:1-13). The pastor must give himself to the main duties of prayer and ministry of the Word (see Acts 6:4). He needs the help and counsel of other wise men.

The wives of the pastor and deacons have an important place of helper to their husbands. Their personal and home lives must be equally exemplary (see 1 Tim. 3:11). There are also single adults who dedicate themselves to be the servants of the church (see 1 Cor. 7:34; Rom. 16:1-2).

AUTHORITY ON A LARGER SCALE

When society grew to a certain stage, God delegated some of His authority to human government. God knew that to keep order in society as we related to each other, there had to be guidelines. And there had to be someone—an authority—to enforce them. Romans 13:4 says the one God puts in charge of keeping order in society is "God's minister, an avenger to execute wrath on him who practices evil."

We are charged to be subject to the higher powers or rulers. In verse 6 we are also told to pay our taxes so that government might be able to function efficiently. It is God who has placed those in charge of society that we might live "quiet and peaceable lives" (1 Tim. 2:2).

We see many abuses in government today, but we could not be so foolish as to abolish the authority of government because of the personal abuses of some. Indeed we must work to correct abuses.

There are different types of human government. A few of them are:

REPUBLIC—a government in which supreme power resides in a body of citizens entitled to vote and is exercised by elected officers and representatives responsible to them and governing according to law

MONARCHY—a government that has undivided rule or absolute sovereignty by a single person

OLIGARCHY—a government in which a small group exercises control, especially for corrupt and selfish purposes

DICTATORSHIP—a form of government in which absolute power, often oppressive or contemptuously overbearing toward others, is concentrated in a dictator or a small clique

COMMUNISM—a totalitarian system of government in which a single authoritarian party controls state-owned means of production with the professed aim of establishing a classless society

We could debate the worth of each type of government and its economic system. This lies outside the purpose of this book, but the bottom line is whether those in charge are godly or wicked.

We in the United States look with disdain upon a dictatorship. We see it as oppressive. There is a tendency to oppression with those who have total power. But there is also the danger of the misuse of democracy. If the people are wicked, they will elect wicked leaders. They will pass wicked laws and judge unjustly. This type of government also can be unbearable. There must be godly rulers, or all human government will be a failure. God's Word says, "When the righteous are in authority, the people rejoice; but when a wicked man rules, the people groan" (Prov. 29:2).

Since I live in a country that is a republic, I have a voice in my government. It is my responsibility to help right the wrongs. This is my country, and working through its established system, I can make it a better place.

THE WAY UP IS DOWN

How are you chosen for one of God's delegated leadership positions? It is so simple that most people miss it. You're in training now. You learn how to be "in charge" by learning how to be obedient. You can't be over unless you're under.

When you were in school and the teacher would leave the room for a short time, she would leave someone "in charge," a monitor. Did she choose the class rowdy? No, she chose someone who obeyed the rules. So God is looking for someone who delights in obeying the rules. He's not looking for someone who wants to boss others around.

In the spiritual realm the way up is down. The way to rule is by being a servant. If God wants to place us in a larger sphere of influence, that's His business. Our job is to be obedient and contented where we are. Do you remember Joseph, who was sold into slavery by his brothers? Joseph was a faithful servant. In God's timing he was promoted to a high place of honor and influence (see Gen. 45:4-5). Peter states the same principle this way, "Humble yourselves under the mighty hand of God that He may exalt you in due time" (1 Peter 5:6).

God's Word says I am to be a servant. I can't do my own self-centered thing. I am a dependent, not an independent person. I must glorify God by obeying Him and serving my fellowman. It doesn't make me a weakling to recognize that without Him "I can do nothing" (John 15:5b). On the contrary, "I can do all things through Christ who strengthens me" (Phil. 4:13).

I'm not exempt from dealing with the heartbreaking problems and the unmerciful storms breaking up homes and wrecking lives. I am a servant. You are a servant. We are God's servants! We should give our lives to relieving human heartbreak, but knowing that "it is not I but Christ" pointing men and women, boys and girls to the Word of God.

I've seen the heartbreak that sin can bring. I've counseled teenage alcoholics. I've prayed with a young lady on the brink of divorce. I've held someone in my arms as she sobbed out her heartbreak over a husband who had just walked out.

I've also seen the healing that God can bring. I've witnessed someone who was heartbroken lean totally on Jesus and His Word. Yes, I've witnessed a miracle. I've seen a home put back together. I've seen changed lives. I've seen someone go to God's Word and claim promise after promise. I've seen these promises fulfilled. What a blessing to be a part of a miracle! I helped pray. I helped encourage that one to look to Jesus, because frankly I had no help to give of my own. I want to be an obedient servant, looking to Jesus and helping others when the storms of life come.

FOR SUCH A TIME

We do not know when God will call upon us to be "in charge." We must be pure and obedient before Him at all times, so when He speaks our names, we won't have to look around and ask, "Who, me?"

Queen Esther was a wonderful example of a gracious lady who recognized her queenly position. She knew her privileges and limitations as the queen. When her Uncle Mordecai asked that piercing question, "Who knows whether you have come to the kingdom for such a time as this?" (Est. 4:14), she had to stop and consider the answer. The whole Jewish nation was in danger of being annihilated.

She did have access to the king, the chief authority. She was a submissive wife. He loved and admired her greatly, but according to the custom of that day, she couldn't simply tap on the throne room door, peek in, and say, "It's your lover girl just stopping by to ask you a question." Without an appropriate invitation, she could be put to death. But she was prepared, and she was courageous. There must have been something about the regal way she stood, the care with which she had prepared her appearance, and the attitude she conveyed that won his heart.

We can only imagine the times she spent alone with God as she yielded her personal rights to her Heavenly King and sought His strength. She fasted and asked others to join her in this God-given assignment. But it wasn't only that day that she prepared herself to gain an audience with the king. It was her daily habit. The king knew her for who she was. With her character established, having prepared herself for the immediate occasion, and being dependent on God, she determined to wield her influence. This matter was so strategically important that she was willing to die. I wonder, will we be prepared like Esther to risk our lives for such a time as this? We've been in training. Will we pass the test?

THE ONLY PERFECT AUTHORITY

God has ordained authority in our lives. But no human authority is perfect. At some time we will be disappointed by our mother or father, our husband, some government official, or even our pastor.

We should be able to expect a higher standard of those who lead us. The king portrayed in Psalm 45:4 is pictured in this fashion: "And in Your majesty ride prosperously because of truth, humility, and righteousness." Isaiah 52:11 says, "Be clean, you who bear the vessels of the LORD."

Likewise, a stricter accountability will be held for those who are teachers. "Let not many of you become teachers, brethren, knowing that as such we shall incur a stricter judgment" (James 3:1 NASB).

Even King David, known as "a man after God's own heart," slipped into serious sin. He let his family down. He let his nation down. Most of all, he let his God down. But David repented, and God forgave him and continued to use him, although he was not spared the dire consequences of his sin.

Nevertheless, we should not be devastated if our leaders make mistakes. We are to keep "Looking unto Jesus, the author and finisher of our faith" (Heb. 12:2). Only God is perfect, and we cannot expect others to "play God" in our lives. Many times we expect too much and then feel let down when those we love and look up to let us down.

WHO YOU ARE

You are the One in whom
I find no fault;
All my expectations
*   are fulfilled in You.*

You always keep
*   Your word;*
You understand my
*   every need.*
You desire to spend
*   Your time with me.*
You remember
*   the words,*
*   the dreams we share.*

Your gentleness and
*   kindness soothe*
*   my troubled brow.*
You long to share
*   with me*
*   Your life and love.*

You want me to understand
*   Your ways.*

You are my beloved
*   and I am Yours.*

I thank You that all I ever dreamed of
in a lover and a leader
are perfected in You.
You are my All in All.

PRAYING FOR THOSE IN AUTHORITY

Therefore I exhort first of all that supplications, prayers, intercessions, and giving
of thanks be made for all men, for kings and all who are in authority, that we may
lead a quiet and peaceable life in all godliness and reverence. For this is good and
acceptable in the sight of God our Savior. (1 Tim. 2:1-3)

It's hard enough to be under the authority of another. Sometimes it becomes almost unbearable if those in authority are unjust, unreasonable, and unloving. I submit to you that prayer is one of the best ways to bring about needed changes. You may not think that this is a concrete enough solution, but it is a method of which God highly approves. Let me close this section by sharing some ways you can pray for both your husband and all those in authority over you.

Spiritually

If he isn't saved, pray for his salvation—not so life will be easier for you, but because you desire his spiritual welfare. If he is saved, pray for his spiritual growth. Pray that he will be a man of wisdom, humility, prayer, and compassion. Pray that he will be a Spirit-filled man of God, laying down his rights and learning to take up his cross daily and follow Jesus. If he has a place of leadership in the church, pray for him to be faithful in that position.

Physically

Pray that he will exercise discipline in the care of his body— in the things he eats and his exercise. Pray for God-given strength in these areas. You can "put feet to your prayers" by fixing nutritious meals and providing an example in the care of your own body.

Mentally

Pray that he will be mentally alert and knowledgeable in the areas relevant to his life. Pray about the books and magazines he reads, the TV programs he watches, so that his mind will remain pure.

Emotionally

Pray for emotional strength to withstand the pressures that come to him from his job, from his peers, family, and financial conditions. Pray that he will be sensitive to the needs of those with whom he works, lives, and comes in contact.

Family Life

Pray that he will take the spiritual leadership of your home, that he will take a vital part in teaching the children about the things of God. Pray that he will be an example and a witness to his family. Pray that he will give proper time to his family and that he will teach the right values and priorities by word and example.

Job-related Relationships

If he is a boss, pray for his ability to administrate, to be fair and sensitive to the needs of his employees. If he is an employee, pray for his diligence, loyalty, and example. If he has a secretary, pray for her and his relationship to her.

Social Relationships

Pray for his example and testimony in day-to-day relationships—on the golf course, the tennis court, at the bowling alley, etc. Pray that he will be gracious and courteous, exhibiting an attitude of gentleness like his Savior. One of my favorite Scriptures says, "His gentleness hath made me great" (Ps. 18:35b).

If we only pray and are not obeying God's commandments to us, God will not pay attention to our prayers. But if we are obedient and add to this our earnest prayers, God will be faithful to hear and answer our persistent prayers for all those in authority over us. From the foot of God's throne we will be exerting the influence He has ordained for us.

PART THREE

Wisely Influencing

10

Biblical Mothers

Her children rise up and call her blessed;
Her husband also, and he praises her.

PROVERBS 31:28

I, as a woman who seeks constantly after wisdom, can have eternal influence. When I am loyal, diligent, and trustworthy, I can be delegated vast areas of responsibility. In our home I keep the checkbook, I spend most of the money and buy most of the food, furnishings, and clothing. For almost fifty years I have had the major, daily oversight of our home and of our children. I am a valuable associate to my husband. When I work under his direction, I can have a vast amount of influence and authority. I have access to give him counsel if I am wise. I can make him happy and help him to be productive.

I have helped set the values for four children. None of them is perfect, but how I praise God for each of them. They accepted Christ when they were young and are all endeavoring to serve Him. My two daughters, Gayle and Janice, are godly homemakers. My oldest son, Steve, is in the ministry of music, and my son, David, is a career missionary.

This generation has demeaned motherhood and confused young women as to the importance of this role. But how grateful I am that for nearly five decades I have had the privilege of being a mother. I cannot begin to tell you how many hours I've spent holding my babies, singing to them and telling them how I loved them and how Jesus loved them. I didn't keep an account of the hours I spent reading to them from the Bible and books about the Bible.

I don't know how many hours I've spent carpooling and making trips to piano lessons. And God only knows the hours I've spent in prayer, talking to my heavenly Father about my children. I postponed taking voice and piano lessons myself. There wasn't time or money for me to add them to the list. Although I wrote a few things and filed them in a drawer, I never had time even to think that one day I might write a book. Many days were so mundane that I forgot to recognize the influence I was having on the world. You see, greatness is built from the blocks of daily faithfulness to the task at hand.

There is a description of the king's daughter in Psalm 45. It says that she is all glorious within and that her clothing is interwoven with gold. Then it says in verse 16, "Instead of Your fathers shall be Your sons, Whom You shall make princes in all the earth." I see in this passage the influence of a mother. She had the responsibility of making her sons princes in all the earth. She could so train them that they would one day be in positions of authority. What a privilege!

Thank You for Letting Me Be Your Mother

On Mother's Day a number of years ago all of my children were home. Only my oldest son was married at the time, and we had only one grandchild. I decided to write each of them a little thank-you note for letting me be their mother. After lunch all of the family gathered in the family room, and I read each note to each child and then one to my husband. The notes were never intended to be read by anyone else, but to let you know what a privilege I count it to be a mother, I have included these "love notes" with the permission of each family member.

FOR STEPHEN

*I was only twenty-one
when you came
into my life—
Much too young to know
what mothering
was all about.
But you taught me
and I loved it.*

*You were curious and
an excellent student;
You loved numbers
and Lincoln Logs.*

You were all boy!
You loved to run
    and play ball;
But still you had
    a gentle side.

A song was in your soul
    when you were just
    a little boy.

Today you are a man,
    with wife and baby
    of your own.
Instead of nursery rhymes
    and building blocks
    for you,
You have Renae to play
    and sing with.
You're building a
    home of your own.

You've shared your
    song with me;
You're producing music
    to bless others
    for the Lord.

Stephen: Your name means "crowned one."
You have caused us to rejoice!
May you be a crown to your Savior—
"Crowned with glory and honor."

I only pray that your keen mind
    be used to reason for your Lord,
That your song be sung for Him,
That you desire to know Him who
    truly knows you.
Thank you for letting me be your mother!

To Gayle

A little girl with big brown eyes—
    you came into my life

And wrapped your arms around my neck
and your love around my heart.

You also loved to run and play
and ride high upon the swing.
With trombone in hand you marched
and played your song.

You loved to draw and had quite
an artistic flair,
But where you most excelled was
with your table tennis racket in your hand.

You've grown up to be a beauty;
You think just like your dad.
You have talents for writing and
for teaching too.

Your quick wit keeps us all
in stitches.
The future lies before you.
May God lead you in the
days ahead.
You are my prophetess
with keen insight from the Lord.

Gayle: Your name means "source of joy."
May your logical mind and quick
wit be used to bring life and
joy to those around you.

May your able tongue be given
over to teaching the Word of God
and counseling those who are
wandering and confused.
Thank you for letting me be your mother!

FOR DAVID

With great anticipation I waited
for your birth.
It was the first time I had a
little nursery.

You were a quiet child,
but I discovered that although you
weren't always talking,
You were always listening and
learning.

With your keen mind
you studied maps and
zip code books.
You loved to read anything
from the Bible to encyclopedias.

When you were just seven,
you read the Bible through.
You learned the books of the Bible
forward, then backward.

When you were eleven, God spoke to you
about being a missionary,
But that was laid aside for other
ambitions, until God spoke His "word"
again to you at camp a few years back.

You took piano as a little boy,
then laid it aside;
But God wouldn't let you forget the song
He placed within your heart.
So in these past few years the music and
the message flow as your heart
sings unto God, with guitar in hand.

That missions call can be heard loud
and clear as even now you prepare
to go to speak His Word around the world.

David: Your name means "beloved."
You are beloved by us and God;
You are chosen to share His Word.
God holds the secret as to how and where.
Be obedient to every command.
He will do the rest!
Thank you for letting me be your mother!

TO JANICE

Last, but not least,
* you came into my life*
* a month early,*
And now you are an early riser.

You loved to sing and play and draw
* bright and happy and unusual things.*
* (Remember the snorks!)*

You've been quite a student.
* You wanted to please,*
* and pleasing you are.*

You are a "dreamer," a "romantic."
* You love to search the Scriptures*
* for symbolic meanings.*
* You love to praise, even when*
* things go wrong.*
Music flows through your
* fingers and your voice.*

Janice: Your name means "gracious gift,"
* and indeed you are to me.*
May your love for people
* provide many opportunities*
* to share the love of Jesus.*

May your love for music be
* used to praise His holy name.*
May your keen mind and ability to write
* be used to communicate*
* salvation's plan.*
Thank you for letting me be your mother!

TO PHILIP

You were my little son, whom God used
* so much in my life.*
You were a beautiful baby;
You were loved by us all.
You had added so much to our lives,
* but God had a special plan for you.*

He had a special home where He
wanted you to live.
When He called, "Philip,"
you answered, "Yes, Lord!"

He's invited us all to come and
live with you and Jesus.
He's preparing a huge mansion
for all of us there.

You were with me only a
few brief months,
But you taught me the greatest
lesson I've ever learned—
to totally depend on Jesus.

I didn't understand it then;
I know I will one day.
But I've been able to comfort many
who were sad, dear Philip—
all because of you.
Thank you for letting me be your mother!

TO ADRIAN

You, who first dropped love notes by my desk,
who walked me home from school,
who first held my hand,
And promised to love 'til death do us part.

First it was one baby,
then two and three,
then four and five.

You've loved me, and you've
loved each child.
You were my lover, my husband,
then a father to my "brood."

Adrian: Your name means "creative one."
I pray God will continue
to use your life
to create love and

> *unity and faith.*
> *Thank you for letting me be a mother!*

I cannot begin to tell you what a privilege it is to be a mother. I cannot begin to tell you what a lie of Satan's it is that children are a curse, so much that many in this generation murder them in the womb. It is Satan's lie that children prevent us from finding career fulfillment. Indeed they are one of the means God has provided for our fulfillment. It is Satan's lie that they keep us from affording the luxuries of this world. Indeed they are the greatest of earthly treasures—one of the few treasures we can take with us to heaven.

Oh, I didn't say they weren't hard work, that they didn't involve sacrifice, tears, and plenty of the mundane. But nothing, *absolutely nothing*, is gained in this life without hard work and sacrifice.

Yes, sometimes I've felt lonely, unappreciated, and frustrated. But I never thought I had a second-rate job. I believe my influence has helped our children and others to know and love Jesus Christ. God only knows the power of a woman's influence when she serves under authority.

Not Totally Responsible

As parents, you and I have a tremendous responsibility to train our children. But we must realize that each child has a will of his or her own. Even if raised in a godly manner, the child can choose to do wrong. Adam and Eve lived in a perfect environment with God, their heavenly Father, as their teacher. They chose to sin. Did God fail? ". . . though I taught them, rising up early and teaching them, yet they have not listened to receive instruction" (Jer. 32:33).

You and I can be partly to blame for our children's failures if we did not train them correctly. But we may not be to blame either. They may have known what was right and chosen the wrong instead. We as parents do have a heavy responsibility but not the total responsibility. They have the responsibility to choose to practice what they have been taught.

WOMEN OF INFLUENCE

Recently I undertook a study on the lives of the kings of Israel and Judah. I'm not a history buff, so I can easily get bogged down in too many historical details. But I'm a people-oriented person, and I was attracted to the attitudes, actions, and reactions of the characters of the story. I underlined the different kings and the key passages that indicated the secret to their success or failure.

I especially noticed the names of women who had influence on their sons and husbands. The names of the wives and mothers were not always mentioned in the historical record, so one should take note when a woman's name appears. Some women influenced their men greatly for evil. Rehoboam's mother was mentioned in 2 Chronicles 12:13-14: "And his mother's name was Naamah an Ammonitess. [Then it follows:] And he did evil, because he did not prepare his heart to seek the Lord."

Asa had to remove his mother, Maachah, from being queen because she had made an idol in a grove. Then it was said of King Jehoram of Judah that "he walked in the way of the kings of Israel, just as the house of Ahab had done, for he had the daughter of Ahab as a wife; and he did evil in the sight of the Lord" (2 Chron. 21:6).

Then there was King Ahaziah, king of Judah, whose mother, Athaliah, "advised him to do wickedly" (2 Chron. 22:3). What an indictment! And we all know of Jezebel, the wife of Ahab, who plotted evil for her husband against Naboth (see 1 Kings 21:5-15). Oh, the powerful influence of a woman for evil.

But there was a flip side as well. The mother of King Uzziah had a positive influence. Her name was Jecoliah of Jerusalem. And the chronicler records that her son did right in the eyes of the Lord (see 2 Chron. 26:4). King Lemuel's mother is another good example. She taught him to expect in a woman the example described in Proverbs 31. What an influence for good she has been through the ages.

And then there was the influence of a mother on the boy king Joash. "Joash was seven years old when he became king. . . . His mother's name was Zibiah of Beersheba. . . . And Joash did what was right in the sight of the Lord" (2 Chron. 24:1-2). "Amaziah was twenty-five years old when he became king, and he reigned twenty-nine years in Jerusalem. His mother's name was Jehoaddan of Jerusalem. And he did what was *right* in the sight of the Lord" (2 Chron. 25:1-2, italics mine).

In other books of the Bible as well, the woman has been used to represent good or evil. In the book of the Revelation it is a woman, pictured as the mother of harlots, who is portrayed as the epitome of evil (see Rev. 17:5). "The woman was arrayed in purple and scarlet, and adorned with gold and precious stones and pearls, having in her hand a golden cup full of abominations and the filthiness of her fornication. I saw the woman, drunk with the blood of the saints and with the blood of the martyrs of Jesus" (Rev. 17:4, 6a).

On the other hand, throughout Proverbs wisdom is portrayed as a woman who beckons to all that is right and good. "Does not wisdom cry out, and understanding lift up her voice? She takes her stand on the top of the high hill, beside the way, where the paths meet. She cries out by the gates, at the entry of the city, at the entrance of the doors. . . . All the words of my mouth are with righteousness; nothing crooked or perverse is in them. . . . Hear instruction and be wise, and do not disdain it" (Prov. 8:1-3, 8, 33).

I want my influence to count for good—not evil. I want my children to rise up and call me blessed and my husband to praise me (Prov. 31:28). What a joy and reward that will be.

AN EXCEPTIONAL EXAMPLE

Mary, the mother of Jesus, could rightly be called "The Woman Who Has Most Influenced the World." A woman chosen by God to conceive the Son of God—to bear Him, to cradle Him in her arms, to nurture and train Him, and then to give Him up to the whole world.

Evangelical Christians have long neglected the example of Mary, probably because of the overemphasis and even the misrepresentation of Mary by some. However, she is a role model for any woman who wants to be an influence for God.

Mary's Word from God

The angel brought a greeting to Mary from God: "Rejoice, highly favored one, the Lord is with you; blessed are you among women!" (Luke 1:28). Or in modern terms: "Hello, Mary, you're special to God." What would be your reaction to such a greeting by an angel? I'm sure yours would be the same as Mary's—she was troubled. "But when she saw him, she was troubled at his saying, and considered what manner of greeting this was" (Luke 1:29).

To relieve her fears he immediately replied, "Do not be afraid, Mary, for you have found favor with God. And behold, you will conceive in your womb and bring forth a Son, and shall call His name Jesus. He will be great, and will be called the Son of the Highest; and the Lord God will give Him the throne of His father David. And He will reign over the house of Jacob forever, and of His kingdom there will be no end" (Luke 1:30-33).

Mary clearly received a word from God through the angel. But God didn't call on Mary to have blind faith. What if He had given her no word, and she simply started gaining weight? What if one day she felt movement in her body, and finally she delivered a baby? What a frightening experience it would have been. For such an unusual circumstance God sent an unusual messenger. Mary received a word from God.

Our Word from God

But how are you and I going to receive a word from God? Should we expect an angel's visit? For a virgin birth, I would say yes. But for your circumstances and my circumstances, I would answer no. How does God speak today? Through His written Word, through sanctified common sense or wisdom, through circumstances, through the counsel of godly people, through the inner voice of the Holy Spirit.

When my son David was overseas as a missions volunteer on Operation Mobilization's missionary ship, the *Doulos*, I was concerned for his welfare—physically, emotionally, and spiritually. In my daily study of God's Word I was reading Psalm 25. Verses 12 and 13 said, "Who is the man that fears the Lord? Him shall He teach in the way He chooses. He himself shall dwell in prosperity." In the center column of my Bible the note interpreted the last part, "shall lodge in goodness." When I read that, God spoke to my heart and used that phrase "lodge in goodness" to visualize for me that David was dwelling in God's goodness, even though he was half a world away. I cannot convince you that God spoke to my spirit. But I know, because peace flooded my soul. I knew in my mind that God was watching over my son, but His Word made that truth real to my spirit by His Spirit.

Another way I can hear God's voice is through a subject study concerning a specific need in my life. I remember one time when I needed strength and comfort. I looked up the words *strength* and *comfort* in my concordance and read all the verses listed. The ones God spoke to my heart I highlighted with a colored pencil. I am using another Bible now, but I can still look through my old Bible and quickly find those verses God gave to me during that time of need. They are highlighted in purple.

Prepared to Receive God's Word

Why do you think Mary so easily received God's word to her? I believe she had a prepared heart. Luke 1:28 and 30 say she was "highly favored." I like what the center-column reference in my Bible says this means: graciously accepted! God had been observing Mary. He knew who she was. He called her name. He knew what she was—a virgin.

Mary was one of five women in the genealogy of Jesus in Matthew 1:1-17. The forgiveness and love of God extended to Tamar—a victim of incest, Rahab—a harlot, Bathsheba—an adulteress, and Ruth—a heathen.

For this task God had to have a virgin. Not that Mary was sinless as some have declared her to be, for in verse 47 she said, "My spirit has rejoiced in God, my Savior." She needed a Redeemer also. But Mary was a virgin with a heart for God, prepared to receive this word when it came.

Mary must have believed the promises concerning the Messiah, because she didn't ask why. She had only one question, an honest question. How? "How can this be, since I do not know a man?"

Most of us would have asked why. "Why me, Lord?" Isn't that the first question we usually ask when some earth-shaking experience happens to us? "Why, why, Lord? Why did this happen to me? I just don't understand. If I only understood why, then I could handle it."

Mary had an honest question, "How can this be, since I do not know a man?" God, through the angel Gabriel, gave her an honest answer: "with God nothing will be impossible" (Matt. 19:26b). Some things God wants us to understand, but He never wants us to question His love, His wisdom, and His judgment.

I have asked God "why" many times. But when my baby Philip was suddenly taken into the presence of God, I didn't cry, "Why me?" Instead I asked, "How should I deal with this grief in my life?" That was the right question. And, as I've already shared, God showed me how to face this grief in a way that brought Him honor.

The Will Relinquished

It was God's will for Mary to conceive in her womb a son by the Holy Ghost. Did she have a choice? Yes. "Then Mary said, 'Behold the maidservant of the Lord! Let it be to me according to your word'" (Luke 1:38a). In other words, "Yes, Lord. I'm available to do Your will, just like You said." She had to choose His will for her life.

Our generation has distorted God's original design for freedom of choice. Today many outspoken, misguided individuals claim it means freedom to kill or not to kill one's unborn child. God gave us the freedom to choose right or wrong. However, we will be accountable for our choices.

FREE TO CHOOSE

She was free to choose
to do His will or not—
Free to live a normal life,
to marry Joseph,
to bear his sons
and daughters.

But she was also free to choose
to give her body
yielded to His will—
Yes, to bear a Son
who bore the likeness
of His Heavenly Father.

She was free to choose—
to reject God's invitation,
to maintain her reputation,
to forget the angel's salutation,
to ignore mankind's salvation!

But she was also free to choose
a life of full submission
according to His Word,
a faith in God
in whom all things
are possible.

She was free to choose,
and so are we.
God, take my life
and overshadow me
with Your dear Spirit.
Be born in me today—and grow.

I'm yielded to Your will—
"Be it unto me according
to Your Word."

This generation of upbeat women, who call themselves feminists, look upon this submissive attitude as demeaning. But in submission lies one of the secrets of becoming a great influence for God. A synonym for submission is meekness. And just think of the blessings God has promised the meek: "Blessed are the meek, for they shall inherit the earth" (Matt. 5:5). "The humble He guides in justice, and the humble He teaches His way" (Ps. 25:9).

Worship Released

Mary made another choice as well. She chose to worship God right then and there, before the performance came (see Luke 1:46-47). She had believed (past tense). There shall be a performance (future tense). In Mary's eyes it was already done. "He that is mighty has done (past tense) great things for me, and holy is His name" (Luke 1:49).

Many years ago I discovered that trusting Jesus, the living Word of God, joined with the written Word of God, releases the worship of God. Sometimes worship is simply a natural outflow of our lives—something we feel like doing. But whether we feel like it or not, we must worship God. How wonderful it is when our worship is a natural overflow of our lives, an expression of our faith in God, a heartfelt indication of our highest calling.

The Work That Resulted

The angel didn't stay and hold Mary's hand. He didn't come back every night to reassure her. "And the angel departed from her" (Luke 1:38b). She was left with only a word from God. She had to hold onto that.

God also gave a "word" to Joseph, assuring him of Mary's genuine love and commitment to him. God is not unreasonable in His demands (see Matt. 1:19-20). Then to Mary, who believed God's promises, came the day for the performance of God's word. "Blessed is she who believed, for there will be a fulfillment of those things which were told her from the Lord" (Luke 1:45).

Do you have a word from God? Has your "angel" left, and you are holding only a word from God? Are you believing God? I'm holding onto some words from God in behalf of my children, my husband, my friends, and those to whom I'm ministering. I've dated them in my Bible. I review them from time to time, memorize them, believe them, claim them—remind God about them! Recently, after many years, I saw a performance of one of those words from God. Now I can see that it has been worth all the prayer, all the concern, all the faith, and all the time invested in believing God's Word and praising Him while I waited on Him to deliver what He had promised me.

The influence of Mary will be felt through all eternity. How grateful I am that a young virgin maiden had so prepared her heart that she heard God's word, that she believed God's word. God only knows the influence my life or your life can have if we will hear and believe God's word to us and say, "Yes, Lord, I'm available!"

Mary, the Model Mother

We have already seen what an example Mary was in submission to God's Word that she would bear His Son. I also believe that she was the model mother.

SHE ROCKED THE CRADLE

She rocked the cradle of the
One who ruled the world,
held Him in her arms,
watched Him grow
from day to day.

She was the one who taught
Him how to read,
to make His bed,
pick up His toys,
kneel down to pray.

He was subject to her
until the time appointed,
And then she let Him go.
He then took control—
Became the Master
of the wind and sea,
Conquered death and hell,
Became my Lord
and hers.

This woman who rocked
the cradle of the
One who ruled
the world.

A Mother's Obedience

The first quality we observe in Mary as the mother of Jesus is her obedience. The angel had told her before Jesus was conceived in her womb that she was to name her baby Jesus. She obeyed this command. Also she obeyed the command for her baby to be circumcised on the eighth day. "And when eight days were completed for the circumcision of the Child, His name was called Jesus, the name given by the angel before He was conceived in the womb" (Luke 2:21).

The law of Moses had a commandment in reference to Mary's purification. She obeyed this command. "Now when the days of her purification according to the law of Moses were completed, they brought Him to Jerusalem to present Him to the Lord (as it is written in the law of the Lord, every male who opens the womb shall be called holy to the Lord)" (Luke 2:22-23).

There was a special law that pertained to the presentation of Jesus to God. A sacrifice was to be made in His behalf. She obeyed this law "to offer a sacrifice according to what is said in the law of the Lord, 'A pair of turtle-doves or two young pigeons'" (Luke 2:24).

A Mother's Blessings

Blessing always follows obedience. As Mary was in the process of obeying the law as it pertained to her new baby boy, a devout man named Simeon was led by the Spirit into the Temple. He took the baby Jesus up in his arms and, first of all, blessed God, for "it had been revealed to him by the Holy Spirit that he would not see death, before he had seen the Lord's Christ" (Luke 2:26).

Then Simeon blessed them, and said to Mary His mother, "Behold, this Child is destined for the fall and rising of many in Israel, and for a sign which will be spoken against (yes, a sword will pierce through your own soul also), that the thoughts of many hearts may be revealed" (Luke 2:34-35).

Each child given to us is a miracle from God, though not in the same way as was Mary's miracle child. We too should make our presentation of that gift back to God. I have done that with each of my children.

I have received untold blessings in the process of raising my children. I have had the blessing of seeing each of them trust Christ as personal Savior and be baptized. I have seen God use each child's unique personality and gifts to be a blessing to others. I am blessed as I hear them play the piano and the guitar as instruments of praise to God, give wise counsel, take charge in a crisis, teach the Word of God, teach their own children to sing and memorize Scripture. I am blessed to see their talents exhibited in countless ways.

A Mother's Sorrow

Mary's blessing also contained a sword of sorrow, for one day her Son would be given up to die for the sins of the world. Likewise, every mother's blessing contains a sword in her soul. For with motherhood comes heartache. When your child suffers heartbreak, you will too. It will be a double grief because of your love for him or her. I know, for I've been there.

John's Gospel tells us, "There stood by the cross of Jesus His mother." Let's stand with Mary at the cross. Imagine what you would feel if Jesus were your son—and He had done no wrong. Yes, how apt the words of Simeon, "(yes, a sword will pierce through your own soul also), that the thoughts of many hearts may be revealed" (Luke 2:34).

One day my husband and I rode from the airport with a worn-out-looking taxi driver who had a son in prison. She said she didn't go to church because for twelve years she had visited her son in prison on Sundays. She was a mother with a sword in her heart. Before we left, we paused and prayed with her for her and her son. Even now we pray, "Oh, God, please send someone to water the seed that was planted. Heal her broken heart and save her and her wayward son."

A Mother's Ponderings

Every godly mother has the same concern for her child—a concern for the child's safety and well-being. We see Mary's concern revealed when she lost Jesus in the Temple when He was twelve years old. Supposing He was among the other travelers, Mary and Joseph went a whole day's journey before they realized that Jesus was missing. After three days they found Him in the Temple talking to the doctors of the Law. Although Mary and Joseph were amazed, her motherly concern was evident: "and His mother said to Him, 'Son, why have You done this to us? Look, Your father and I have sought You anxiously'" (Luke 2:48).

Jesus replied that He was busy about His Father's business (see Luke 2:49); His parents didn't understand this comment. Mary stored this in her "computer." She "kept all these things and pondered them in her heart" (Luke 2:19).

Mary didn't understand many things in regard to her Son right away, and neither will we understand many things regarding our children. But we should follow Mary's example as we ponder many circumstances in our hearts.

A Mother's Control

The Bible tells us that after the incident in the temple, Jesus "went down with them, and came to Nazareth, and was subject unto them" (Luke 2:51). Mary took control over the things that were rightfully hers. She left to God the things that were rightfully His. The art of motherhood is to know the difference. Proper parenting is to ponder and pray.

It's not our job to have a will for our child, but to be an avenue to help him or her discover God's will. When Mary said, "Let it be to me according to Your word" (Luke 1:38), it didn't just mean the conception of a child but also the completion of the child.

A Mother Lets Go

Mary, along with Joseph, had the oversight of Jesus, and He was subject to them. Every child must be under the authority of parents to receive God's protection and blessings. But the day comes when we mothers must relinquish this control. It's done more effectively a little at a time from the period they are young until the day they move out of the house. For some mothers sending their baby off to first grade is traumatic. For others it is pure relief. Off to college is definitely a crisis point, as is the child's marriage. A child's moving out of town is a real heartbreaker.

The day I said good-bye to my son David, his wife, Kelly, and seven-month-old Jonathan was the "happiest, saddest day" of my life. They were going to Spain as missionaries, potentially for a lifetime. Yes, it was sad, and the tears flowed amidst the hugs and kisses. But then an indescribable joy flooded my heart just to think that I had a son and a daughter-in-law who loved God so much that they were willing to leave father, mother, houses, and lands to take the Gospel to the people of Spain.

I believe that a crisis point for Mary was at the wedding at Cana. Mary was probably a good planner. She noticed when the refreshments ran out. She went and told Jesus, "They have no wine." Jesus said to her, "Woman, what does your concern have to do with Me?" I think what Jesus was saying was, "Mother, you must stop telling Me what to do." She then told the servants, "Whatever He says to you, do it" (John 2:3-5). In other words, "He's in charge." I believe Mary had this revelation: *Stop giving orders and start taking them.* It's unthinkable that what she told them to do, she was unwilling to do. This was some of the best advice ever given.

The story in Matthew 12:46-50 has always caused a pang in my heart for Mary. That was the occasion when Jesus was told that His mother and brothers were waiting outside to speak with Him. But Jesus replied, "'Who is My mother and who are My brothers?' And He stretched out His hand toward His disciples and said, 'Here are My mother and My brothers! For whoever does the will of My Father in heaven is My brother and sister and mother.'"

Mary's relationship was unique among all other mother-son relationships, but there is some similarity to other mothers and sons. He was her son in the flesh, but He was her Savior spiritually. And spiritually she had no greater place than any other person. She must acknowledge, "My son, the Savior." But she must also confess, "My son, my Savior." He wanted her to recognize the difference. She must not only relinquish control as a mother, but she must recognize His spiritual authority over her.

Likewise, we should affirm our grown children in their roles and treat them with respect. We are training them to take spiritual leadership roles as well as to be mature adults. When this final day comes, what a joy and freedom it is if you have done a good job. Anna Mow said that you've succeeded as a parent when you've worked yourself out of a job, but not out of a relationship.

I have never once missed the days of carpooling. I've never missed refereeing disagreements or reminding my children to clean up their rooms. But I have sorely missed the fellowship of my grown children when they were far away. How thankful I am for the telephone and for the mail service. Last Mother's Day was complete when the last child called to say, "I love you."

While Mary no longer managed Jesus, she still mothered Him. She stood at the foot of His cross and wept. And though she did not outrank you and me spiritually, Jesus cared for her as a mother right up until the end. On the cross He appointed John to watch over her when He was gone (see John 19:26-27).

11

Lessons on Raising Children

Like arrows in the hand of a warrior,
so are the children of one's youth.

PSALM 127:4

Many circumstances and many individuals have contributed to the measure of wisdom I learned to exhibit while I was raising my own children. Most likely you will one day find yourself in the role of mother (if you aren't there now). Perhaps these miscellaneous observations and life lessons will resonate with your circumstances.

THE INFLUENCE OF PRAYER

One important influence that will not end even after your children are grown and out from under your control is the one of prayer. Someone said that at this period of a child's life a parent's motto should be, "Hands off; prayers on; mouths shut; hearts open."

I remember when our oldest son was first married that one Sunday night we came home to find that he and his wife had not gone to church, but were at our house watching television. I felt like marching in and declaring, "If you don't go to church, you can't watch my television." I'm glad I didn't do that. We didn't have a problem with our relationship, so why should I create one? I decided instead to pray.

On their wedding day, I had claimed for them the promises in Psalm 84. I began to intensify my praying for them the promises in verse 4: "Blessed are those who dwell in Your house; they will still be praising You." Today my son is a composer and arranger of music, praising and serving the Lord.

I've had the privilege of praying for my children's mates before they were married. I also have the privilege of praying about their concerns after marriage. I have prayed for hours during their transitional times and new opportunities in vocational guidance. It's so much better to pray than to worry. I've had the privilege of praying for my children in their times of grief and trouble. The tears flowed as I prayed through loss, through miscarriage, broken relationships, and disappointments.

There is joy in answered prayer. I remember holding my grandchild Michael in my arms—an answer to prayer for Gayle and Mike in which I had a vital part. When David returned from two years as a volunteer missionary, I longed that he might meet that helper God had chosen for him. I knew that mother-love only went so far. I've prayed all of his life for that special girl whom God would send, but I intensified my prayers for her during that time.

I didn't ask for someone short or tall, with blue eyes or brown, alto or soprano voice. I didn't request that she could sing or play the piano, that she be rich or pretty. The girl of my prayers was a Proverbs 31 girl—one who loved God and who would love my David, who would build him up, encourage and challenge him as he sought to serve the Lord.

Kelly is the girl of my prayers. She's beautiful inside and out. She loves God and wants to serve Him above all. But her eyes light up when David comes in the room, and David has a glow when she's around.

How I praise God for the far-reaching and continual influence of prayer.

LIFE AS IT IS

I'd like to share with you these excerpts from my journal. Perhaps they will give you a glimpse into the stages of parenting our home has experienced.

Tiny Tots

If life wasn't so ordinary and everyday, it might be amusing. Let me describe the circumstances that surround me at this moment. My house is a complete wreck; my nineteen-month-old son, David, has caused many errors in my typing so far because of his reaching for me. He has a runny nose. He just wants me to hold him. His five-year-old sister, Gayle, is talking incessantly, and it is hard for me to concentrate.

I folded a "mountain" of clothes last night, while catching glimpses of a television program. The diapers are still on the couch. I was just too tired to put them up. The dishes from last night are staring at me too—plus the breakfast dishes. My daughter still lingers at my elbow with this pressing question, "When is Easter?"—which is still a month away. My boy is out of my lap, amused momentarily with a cookie.

Oh yes, I have a three-month-old baby, Janice, who (wonder of all wonders) is quiet at the moment, and a six-year-old son, Steve, who is in the first grade. Last night the nineteen-month-old woke up crying and would have no one but Mama, and the baby woke up for her bottle. Daddy had to come to my assistance, for which I was grateful. Then they both went back to sleep at the same time. This is really life as it is!

Frankly, if someone came to see me right now, I would be downright ashamed to let them in. I do hope no one does, but wouldn't that really be just plain old life?

(To be continued later—as the baby has stopped her amazing quietness. In fact, the nineteen-month-old is rocking the bassinet as he has seen me do.)

I'm back—but it is six years later! I didn't have time to sit down again that day. I put my original piece of paper in a drawer, and it has stayed there six years—along with other quickly scribbled items on various subjects.

I live in a different house now—in a different town. I have a laundry room with drawers to put my folded clothes in until I have time to put them up. I rarely go off if the dishes aren't washed. I also have a dishwasher, and the children are old enough to load it. The majority of the house is usually presentable in case company happens to drop in.

My baby started to school this year. It is quiet around the house—at least until 2 P.M. when school lets out. Life has slowed down somewhat, and I am beginning to find myself again. At times things are busy and at times frustrating, but they are fulfilling.

Tear-Brimmed Eyes

Today my oldest son left for school. He not only left for school, but left by plane for England to be gone for eleven months.

I'm not prone to displays of emotion, but I knew as the days grew nearer, that I would experience something when my number-one son left home. Well, there were the tear-brimmed eyes that spilled over as we watched the steel-girded bird lift its wings and gradually disappear into the clouds.

As the family stood on the observation deck, we all bowed our heads as Dad lifted our hearts to heaven and committed him into the hands of his heavenly Father. I prayed silently, "Oh, God, teach him to do Your will."

How thoughtful of our Father to paint a fantastic sunset as a grand send-off. Perhaps our son didn't see the sunset, for he was flying east; perhaps it was just for us who were left behind—a promise that Jesus would answer that prayer.

Second Child to College

I hadn't prepared myself when my second child left for school. I had known for months that she was leaving, and as the last few weeks and even days drew near, I was very calm and collected.

She was only going to be an hour's drive away, so I hadn't thought about missing her. I would still have two children at home, so I hadn't considered the empty-house feeling.

The day we took Gayle to school was ideal. Everyone was calm and sweet and loving. We helped her move in and stayed until the finishing touches were put on the room. Then we went out for a lovely dinner—treating her to a T-bone steak. The day was climaxed with prayers of dedication as we joined hands with her roommate and her roommate's parents.

I wasn't prepared for the emotional letdown that followed on the next day. That's when it hit me that Gayle was gone—her room was so very clean and so very empty.

I just saw her yesterday. She would be home for the weekend to go to a football game, so I would see her soon. I knew I shouldn't cry, so to compensate I decided to write my son, who lives a long way from home and can't get home for weekends.

Ironically, writing the letter just made me miss my son more than ever. I guess I transferred my emotions about my daughter over to him. The day finally ended, and we went to bed. I couldn't keep myself from thinking about Gayle. I didn't know why I was in the "weepy" mood. Later I realized that it was knowing deep within that a new relationship was beginning. Yes, I would see her often on weekends and vacations, but I knew it would never be the same again.

I really do want to be a successful mother. I want my children to grow up—to be able to make wise decisions on their own. This involves steps toward freedom at the right time. Going to college is one of those right times to aid growing toward maturity. But who said that it wasn't normal to feel a little pain within when the strings of dependence are cut?

I just couldn't contain myself as we tried to go to sleep—so I slipped into the bathroom and closed the door and had a good cry. Then I prayed and committed her to the Lord. Everything seemed better, and I went back to bed and went to sleep.

THE TAMING OF THE WILD OX

The analogy of the "wild ox" is hidden away in a description of the omnipotence of God (Job 39:9-12). The first time I studied this Scripture, my oldest son was overseas at school, preparing to come home. He was at a time in his life of asserting his independence and becoming his own man. Job asks the question: "Will the wild ox be willing to serve you? Will he bed by your manger? Can you bind the wild ox in the furrow with ropes? Or will he plow the valleys behind you? Will you trust him because his strength is great? Or will you leave your labor to him? Will you trust him to bring home your grain, and gather it to your threshing floor?"

God impressed on my heart that day that my son was my "wild ox," wanting to be free to make his own decisions. And the answer to all the questions in the above passage was no. My wild ox would not do any of those things. But the *tame* ox would. Then the Lord assured me: "And I'm the only One who can tame him. I've been *using* you all these years, but today I want to make it very clear, you must trust Me implicitly to complete the job of the 'taming of the wild ox.' If you do, I promise you that I'll do it."

With full assurance I committed the job to God's hands. If there was ever a time that I believed God for anything, it was that day. It's exciting every time I think about it. The Lord has been doing a marvelous job.

Our son came home from school with a desire to help in our ministry. For four months we experienced the fulfillment of the promise God gave to me, as our son made a valuable contribution to our work by eagerly helping in the youth ministry of the church. It was so good to have him home again with a prospect of being with us two more years.

At the end of four months the Lord called us to another state. Since Steve didn't wish to come, we left him behind in college. The Lord knew what He was doing, for our wild ox began to mature and to serve God in a youth ministry uniquely suited to his talents and personality.

He married and moved near us for a couple of years. He visited frequently after that—but on a new basis. His judgments were wiser and his lifestyle maturing. I prayed that he'd love our new home, the church, and friends, and that our family would continue to enjoy one another.

There was an inward rejoicing during those days, as I saw God faithfully fulfilling His promise. I saw evidence of the "taming of the wild ox." Yes, my son is no longer a boy; he is a man. And I like what I see. I clipped strings a little at a time for years. Some were more painful than others, but there was a release and an inward peace. I have great confidence in what God is doing in Steve's unique life.

Practical Pointers for Ox Taming

Listed below are hints that I've found valuable in the taming of four wild oxen. Yes, I have made many mistakes, but with prayer, confession of these mistakes, and many new beginnings, it has been an exciting adventure.

- Receive your basic instruction from God's Word. There is no substitute for a daily searching of the Bible and discovering specific precepts and promises for your child (Deut. 6:6-9). After the study of God's Word, gain insights in training children from Christian books. Be sure to check all the principles in these books by the Word of God (Prov. 11:14).
- Discipline with fairness and consistency. Provide guidelines based on God's Word. Have mercy for genuine repentance. Use physical correction only when other methods won't work. Don't discipline in anger (Prov. 23:13; Eph. 6:4).
- Lead your child to Jesus at an early age and encourage him or her in Christian growth and involvement in service for the Lord (2 Tim. 3:15; Prov. 23:15-16).
- Understand and appreciate the individuality of your child. Help him have a healthy evaluation of his temperament, talents, spiritual gifts, role, and phase of life (1 Cor. 12).
- Recognize the importance of training your child in the ability to make decisions. Release her a little at a time so that when she reaches college age, she will be ready to handle important decisions (Prov. 22:6).
- Teach by example how to confess wrongs and to ask for and to give forgiveness as the way to bring unity between family members, friends, and foes (Eph. 4:32).
- Be available to share in your child's problems and joys, defeats and achievements. Be genuinely interested and always have a listening ear (James 1:19).
- Teach your child to establish priorities and time scheduling (Prov. 23:22-23; Eccl. 12:1).
- Teach responsibility and basic skills. Chores that are appropriate to the age of the child teach the importance of work and will aid in being responsible for all of one's workload later (Prov. 10:5).
- Teach your child to praise the Lord at all times (Ps. 34:1, 3; 90:14).

- Provide training to develop your child's talents. Use books, hobbies, travel, music lessons, swimming or tennis lessons to help discover these areas. Encourage him by rejoicing in his accomplishments (1 Thess. 5:11).
- Teach by attitude, example, and definite instruction an appreciation and respect for the opposite sex (Prov. 23:26-27; 5:18-21).
- Help your child discover God's will for her life. Show her that true fulfillment comes in doing God's will instead of through fame, prosperity, pleasure, or beauty (Eccl. 12:1).
- Show the importance of Bible study, Scripture memory, and, most of all, how to make the Scriptures real and practical for daily living (Ps. 119:9, 11).
- Guide your child in understanding the importance of godly friends (Prov. 1:10, 15; 22:24-25; 23:19-21).
- Set an example of love by loving your husband (Titus 2:4).
- Spend time having fun together—playing games, watching sports, going on picnics, taking trips. Let laughter ring through your home daily (Job 8:21; Ps. 126:2).
- Provide encouragement. Be a motivator. Rejoice in your child's accomplishments and growth in all areas—physical, psychological, and spiritual (Prov. 23:15-16, 24-25).

BEAUTIFUL CONFIRMATION

I had arrived for a three-day stay with my son's future in-laws. A wedding was scheduled in four months, and Tennessee and Florida were pretty far apart for much planning together. While I was there, the future bride and groom were to arrive for a day off from nearby colleges.

The mother and father of the bride were previous acquaintances and fellow church members. It was such a joy to be in their home and to experience the fellowship we had those few days. The mother-in-law, June, graciously shared the plans that were being made and asked for any suggestions. I didn't intend to make a nuisance of myself, so I had not planned any suggestions before I came.

Nevertheless, I was delighted when she invited me to compose the words for the wedding invitation. We thought it would be nice if we based it on a Scripture verse that meant something special. As June and I were sharing one afternoon, a verse came to her that God had shown her several years before and given to her as a promise for her son and daughter: "That our sons may be like plants grown up in their youth; that our daughters may be like cornerstones polished after the similitude of a palace" (Ps. 144:12 KJV).

I was so excited because I had written two poems about that verse several years before. I had written a date in my Bible claiming it as a promise for my sons and daughters.

When Cindi and Steve got home, we were sharing about our verse. They both concluded we should use this verse on the invitation.

The next morning was Sunday. When I awoke, the verse, "Every good gift and every perfect gift is from above" (James 1:17) was on my heart. On the way to church I remarked, "Let me share my verse for today." June had that verse underlined in her Bible too. We rejoiced together that God had made us of one mind and heart. We decided to use that verse at the top of the invitation and Psalm 144:12 at the bottom.

The climax to the weekend came when we gathered around the dining table for prayer before we went to bed. It was such a sweet time as our children thanked the Lord for their parents. Then we all asked God to bless their wedding—which He did, in remarkable ways. But that's a story for another day.

ACROSS THE MILES

My son David has always been the typical calm, cool, and collected type. But in his younger years, he did not show much excitement about any activity. One of the prayers I prayed for him all year was that the Lord would motivate him to action.

He retreated into his room and played his guitar in most of his spare moments. As the years progressed, he expressed an interest in going overseas for the summer with a missions organization called Operation Mobilization. We began to pray that God would lead him in this decision. David felt a confirmation that this was God's will. Quite a large amount of money had to be raised. But he couldn't directly ask for financial support—only for prayer support. It was also specified that he or his family couldn't give over a certain amount. The rest had to come in answer to prayer. He emptied his savings; we gave what we could, and he prayed and waited. At last the day came when all his support was given. How we praised God for answered prayer.

He discovered that those who played the guitar could take their instruments along. I was beginning to see the reason David had been playing his guitar so much. He was able to join a musical group going to Austria for the summer. Some of their witnessing opportunities developed by going door to door singing and playing.

Each day we prayed. How thrilled we were when we heard how God was using David. He described how they went door to door singing, playing, and sharing the Gospel, how they had Bible studies for the local young people.

After two months the day came for him to come back home. We talked for hours that first night. It was a long time before he "ran down." Truly God had motivated David. A vision for reaching people for Christ had been planted in his heart. He still prays for some of his Austrian friends to grow in their knowledge of Christ, though now he is a missionary in Spain with his wife and children.

THE SOUND OF MUSIC

He has put a new song in my mouth—praise to our God; many will see it and fear, and will trust in the Lord. (Ps. 40:3)

Ever since I can remember I have loved to sing. Sometimes it was a hymn sung in church, or other times I would just hum a tune while I worked. It was no wonder when I had my children that the sound of music was heard throughout our home. I sang to them when I rocked them. We sang together as we took walks.

Our youngest daughter, Janice, loved to sit at the piano and play and sing. And I loved to hear her. Janice was a teenager when she first saw the movie *The Sound of Music*. She liked the film and, of course, the music. She played all the songs on the piano and sang until she had memorized them all. The song she loved the most was "My Favorite Things."

Janice trusted Jesus when she was just a little girl and liked to praise the Lord through her music. There were times of tears and heartache—like the time she had to move away from her favorite friend, Jill, and the time when her favorite dog, Tawny, died. Later on as a young woman, she suffered a devastating loss. She combined the melody to this favorite song with her love for Jesus and wrote a song containing these beautiful words:

JOY THROUGH MY TEARDROPS
Joy thru my teardrops, and gains thru my losses
Beauty for ashes, and crowns for my crosses.
He binds my wounds, and He dries all my tears
Calms every storm, and He conquers my fears.

Lord, in the time of deep grief and emotion,
I will yet serve You with constant devotion;
You have not failed me one step of the way.
That is the reason I'll trust You and say:

> *I will praise You! I will praise You!*
> *Jesus Christ, my King;*
> *For You fill my heart with a song in the night.*
> *Yes, You make my heart to sing!*

"LORD, IT WOULD BE REAL NICE!"

Delight yourself also in the Lord, and He shall give you the desires of your heart.
(Ps. 37:4)

I had heard from lots of people that grandmothering is the ultimate in all of this life's experiences. God gave me "the desires of my heart"—the gift of being a grandparent.

My husband and I had ten days' vacation time to wait for our first grandchild. So we boarded the airplane the day after Christmas and headed for Florida. I didn't want to pray selfishly, but I did tell the Lord my desires. I said that it surely would be nice if the baby could be born while we were there.

The weekend came and went and still no baby. We all thought maybe Cindi would have the first baby of the New Year. But New Year's Day came and went and still no baby. But at 4:15 the next morning, a knock came at our bedroom door. Steve said, "We're getting ready to go to the hospital." The first words that came to my mind were "a time to be born" (Eccl. 3:2). We got up, and my husband led in prayer as we all held hands. Then Steve took Cindi to the hospital. I wanted to go too, but this was Steve and Cindi's hour together. We would go to the hospital later.

We were staying with Cindi's parents, so after breakfast we all went to the hospital and waited in the waiting room. The grandparents were allowed to go in to see the baby and the parents for five minutes. The baby was so beautiful. Of course I would think so. I'm her grandmother! We went to the nursery later and looked and looked and took lots of pictures.

Thank you, Lord, for giving me the desires of my heart—to be able to be there when "our" baby was born and to visit with Cindi and Steve and the grandparents-in-law.

Now my husband and I are the proud grandparents of eight grandchildren, with one on the way. It's just my husband and me in our home—the children long gone with their own families to raise. Indeed, my quiver is full!

12

Keeper at Home

There are many commands given to all Christians, but to women God has given one special command. In Titus, the second chapter, verse 5, the apostle Paul says that women are to be "keepers at home." Paul says in 1 Timothy 5:14, "Therefore I desire that the younger widows marry, bear children, manage the house, give no opportunity to the adversary to speak reproachfully."

The traditional male-female roles are being challenged today. There is much confusion and extremism on both sides of the issue. Some want to completely discard the idea of roles. Extremists seek to compensate for the inequities of life by proposing government-funded childcare centers, easy abortions for unwanted pregnancies, and legislation for preferred treatment in job opportunities.

Other extremist groups try to limit the woman's sphere of activity to the home alone, ignoring the fact that scientific advancements have made it possible for her to complete her household duties in less time.

God would like us to have a balanced view somewhere between the two extremes. The wise woman will look at these issues from God's point of view.

If you have chosen marriage, you have already chosen to be a homemaker. Homemaking must be your priority. This does not mean it will consume all your time. How time-consuming homemaking is will vary with the number and ages of your children, the desires of your husband, your physical strength, and your temperament. However, many have given up their responsibility for proper family nutrition and for children's education and spiritual and emotional welfare. We cannot give over these responsibilities to others.

The fulfillment we gain from homemaking depends on our attitude. It needs to be one of contentment. The word *content* comes from a Latin word meaning "to hold together." When we are content, we think clearly, and we remain focused on true values of life. We think, talk, and act in an organized manner.[1]

If we aren't content, we are doubting God's provisions for our happiness. The psalmist expressed it this way: "In the multitude of my anxieties within me, your comforts delight my soul" (Ps. 94:19).

Perhaps the greatest cause for marital unhappiness is discontentment. Some people are always searching for more. They think they will be happy with:

A new husband
> A new baby
>> A new car
>>> A new house
>>>> A better job
>>>>> A bigger house
>>>>>> And on and on!

Contentment doesn't come naturally. Paul said, "I have learned in whatever state I am, to be content" (Phil. 4:11). This learning process involves counting our blessings and focusing on the things we *do* like instead of on the things we *don't* like.

When my husband accepted the pastorate at Bellevue Baptist Church, we moved from Florida to Tennessee. Some folks think Tennessee is the deep South, but as far as I was concerned, it was about as north as it could be. In the winter the state was rainy and cold. Memphis seemed enormous. But I took that Scripture literally, "in whatever state I am." That had to mean Florida or Tennessee. I chose to be content in Tennessee. And I was. The Lord added so many extra blessings to my life that I never would have recognized had I not chosen contentment.

Now the fall is thrilling to me with its magnificent changing of the leaves. After the bleak, cold winter comes the wonder of springtime. I had never experienced these in Florida. Ella May Miller says, "Gratitude is the foundation upon which contentment is built."[2]

SEEING GOD IN THE ORDINARY

Truly there are blessings all around us. God's fingerprints are all over His creation. It is not difficult to marvel at a glorious sunset or stand amazed at the ocean's edge where we can watch those powerful billows roar to a silent stop on the shore. Surely only God could engineer such a feat. When spring is abloom with its magnificent array of flowers—pink and white, yellow and purple—our hearts consciously call out to this God of exquisite beauty.

But do we see God in the ordinary? Often outside the window of my study, I see birds and squirrels feeding on the seeds I've sprinkled there. They all look so ordinary. Yet I've learned to leave my binoculars nearby. When I concentrate on one of these so-called "dull" little creatures, a world of hidden beauty bursts forth. Delicate colors—shades of gray and brown and rust—black markings, white collars, and even bright yellow spots appear when viewed this way. Each of these creatures has markings so delicate and so unique.

The world of the "ordinary" is not so ordinary with God. He has put as much effort in their creation as in the more flamboyant cardinal and blue jay. It is all waiting there for the one who will take the time and effort to see with more than just the naked eye.

The loving expression of a thoughtful God is everywhere. If I can only learn to say, "Thank you, Jesus, for all You have done," He will fill me with inner peace and joy. In Christ I can find the strength to change my wrong attitudes. He can help me organize my thoughts. God cares about my every-day frustrations.

One thing that robs the homemaker of her contentment is the drudgery of her life. Many find the daily chores boring and unchallenging. They think that if they could only rid themselves of the drudgery, life would be satisfying.

Don't forget what God said to Adam and Eve in the Garden of Eden after sin entered their lives. He declared, "Cursed is the ground for your sake" (Gen. 3:17). You may not understand why, but God intended to use the drudgery to work out His will in our lives.

Work comes hand-in-hand with homemaking. But remember, there is no debut of the concert pianist without years of endless scales and finger exercises. There is no successful heart transplant without the years of study and hard routine work. It is by means of drudgery that the spectacular is attained. But don't live for the spectacular. Let God tend to that. Don't despise the household chores. You can make a "little bit of heaven" out of your earthly homes if you will learn to accept God's means of perfecting your life. He can transform your drudgery into joy with His presence.

I don't want to be an ordinary housewife, getting by with as little effort as possible. I want my home to be more than just a place to come for meals and a bed in which to sleep. I want to live creatively even in the ordinary circumstances of life.

SETTING GOALS

A wise homemaker sets challenging goals for herself. You can have desires for your husband and your children, but you can only set goals for yourself. Before you read on, sit down with pen and paper in hand and verbalize your own inner goals. I did this and arrived at these over-arching goals:

- To love Jesus and serve Him faithfully.
- To be content with the possessions I have and the circumstances of my life.
- To provide a creative home atmosphere where the family can enjoy being together and sharing hospitality with our friends.
- To care adequately for my family's physical needs.
- To provide whatever education, training, and encouragement is needed to equip my children for a contented life.
- To use my gifts and talents in a meaningful way.

There can be a variety of outward means to accomplish your goals. You can work out short-range ways to reach these long-range goals. Always have a challenging project that you are working on. Don't be tricked into thinking that you will waste your education if you don't have a paid job outside the home.

The educated mother can better answer the hundreds of daily questions. She can interpret life more intelligently. She can better follow her children in their school and community activities. She can use her knowledge of science or mathematics, her artistic or nursing skills within the framework of her home. If used in the proper way, education can help produce better wives and mothers.[3]

CREATING AN ATMOSPHERE

Speaking to one another in psalms and hymns and spiritual songs, singing and making melody in your heart to the Lord. (Eph. 5:19)

Creative homemaking is so much more than merely providing for the necessities of life. It is wrapped up in the atmosphere that we create. The atmosphere is dependent upon our own attitudes. Are we happy and singing as we work? Are we pleasant and courteous?

Music is one of the best ways to create a joyful atmosphere. Christian records and tapes can be played around the home, starting when the children are young. The hymnbook should have a prominent place. Any interest in music can be encouraged in family members.

We can fill the hearts and minds of our children with challenging Christian books that will give them a burning desire to do God's will for their lives. We can increase our children's Bible knowledge by purchasing Christian coloring books, puzzles, and games. Family worship can be fun and challenging through playing games such as Bible baseball or through Bible drills with the children.

When my children were growing up, I placed Scripture cards at their dinner plates for them to read aloud before we ate. When children get older, they can take turns leading the family devotions. Prayer requests of common interest should be shared by the entire family. Each child should be encouraged to have a personal time of devotions and Scripture memory.

With imagination we can create an atmosphere of faith in which Scripture can be applied to day-by-day experiences. Disappointments can be faced later on in life if we have taught our children an attitude of praise and thanksgiving.

But by far the most important atmosphere that we set for our children is one of love. This is taught more by example than by words, but don't underestimate the necessity for words. Learn to say, "I love you," often.

FAMILY TRADITIONS

Holidays, birthdays, and graduations can all be meaningful times to draw the family closer together. These occasions should be remembered and treasured. While our children were living at home, we inaugurated many family traditions.

On birthdays and graduations our children came to expect a display of pictures and handiwork done by them at various ages. Their individual accomplishments were recognized, and pictures were taken.

On Thanksgiving members of the family came to the dinner table ready to name a specific thing for which they would like to thank the Lord. As they shared the event or person for which they were thankful, they lit a candle on the Thanksgiving wreath, the centerpiece for the table.

The story of the birth of Jesus was, and continues to be, a part of our Christmas celebration. One year verses about giving were placed on the presents; another time a good wish for the next year was given from one family member to another; another time verses from Isaiah, prophesying about Jesus, the Messiah, were read. An open Bible and the manger scene are central in the decorations.

One Easter small objects that symbolized the crucifixion and resurrection stories were placed at each seat at the table. Each person showed his object, told what it represented, and then read the Scripture that was attached. Examples of the objects were nails, a wooden cross, a stone, an angel, and a piece of white cloth.

HOME DECOR—AN EXPRESSION OF FAITH

A home should not be decorated pretentiously to impress other people. It should be designed to be lived in and enjoyed. The decor should express not only our personality and our tastes, but also our faith in Christ. Somewhere there should be expressions that show we know and love our Lord. This doesn't mean we have to have a big picture of Jesus hanging in the living room. The way we express ourselves will be as different as our personalities.

In my home we have placed a crown of thorns on the open pages of a large family Bible. Around the room, worked into our decorations are various treasures collected on a number of trips to the Holy Land. These include an olivewood shepherd with his sheep, a rock from the hill of Calvary, a carving of the two spies returning from Canaan, and pictures of the Holy Land on the walls. Scripture texts are also displayed at our front entrance and throughout the house, and Christian books are on the shelves. Mementos from countries where we have gone to minister for Christ serve to remind us to pray for the peoples of the world.

We have many other items in our decorations, such as paintings of outdoor scenes, flower arrangements, family pictures, and ginger jars. Our colors express our favorites, green and gold, orange and brown. We love the outdoors, so our house has lots of glass so we can see our backyard and neighborhood lake.

Our home isn't filled with extravagant items, but I love it. It reminds me of many lovely memories. Best of all, you can tell that a Christian family lives here.

13

Feeding Her Family

She watches over the ways of her household, and
does not eat the bread of idleness.

PROVERBS 31:27

More than twenty years ago I committed myself to a healthier way of eating. This has involved eliminating some items from my diet, adding others to it, and becoming more conscientious in the buying and preparation of foods. It has been hard work to reprogram lifelong habits and to correct a convenience-prone mind-set. Healthy eating has now become a natural part of my life, and it has been worth every bit of time and energy I have invested.

In fact I feel so deeply about this subject that I have written a book titled *The Bible's Seven Secrets to Healthy Eating.* It's not just another diet book with a "detour to a quick cure." The book is about getting on God's "highway to health" by eating natural, whole foods and following biblical guidelines.

My main purpose has been to make my body a healthier temple for the Holy Spirit to live in. Moderation or self-control is a fruit of the Spirit. Too many modern Christians are gluttonous eaters and are not a good testimony for Christ. They aren't keeping their bodies fit temples for the Holy Spirit.

I've become convinced that every homemaker should become an expert in the field of nutrition. Too many have only a surface knowledge of the subject and are influenced mainly by advertisements and hearsay.

Since changing my eating habits, I've experienced a much greater vitality. I challenge you to search for the truth in this area and then work it out in your own life.

It seems to me that a wise woman will prepare nutritious and appealing meals. While nutritional guidelines often change, some facts remain fixed.

Nutritious meals will include the six nutrients: 1) protein, 2) carbohydrates, 3) fats, 4) vitamins, 5) minerals, and 6) water. These nutrients are present in the foods we eat and contain chemical substances that function in one or more of three ways: They furnish the body with heat and energy, provide material for growth and repair of body tissues, and assist in the regulation of body processes.[1]

In the beginning God provided "naturally nutritious" foods. Big industrial food processors have refined, substituted, and artificially preserved these products. Most of us are uninformed. We blindly trust the government to make sure industry uses nutritious ingredients.

The producer knows that if he keeps food in its natural state, it will spoil within a short time. Therefore, he adds preservatives to his product. Shelf life benefits the food industry and our convenience-prone laziness. For years we have thought the chemicals being added to our food to preserve it were harmless; however, many harmful results have been surfacing in recent years.

Some of the means of preservation are being labeled as cancer-causing. Other means simply rob food of its nutritional value. Some people don't care. Others are oblivious to the whole process.

Don't fall prey to these invisible thieves and silent killers. Whether you understand God's laws or not, they will still operate the way God intended. One of these laws is that correct eating habits promote good health. We can take it upon ourselves to obtain an education and become aware of the positive and negative aspects of nutrition.

The Bible isn't a nutritional textbook, but you may be surprised when you find out that it is filled with admonitions about food. Although not necessary to our salvation, the dietary guidelines given to Israel provide material for thought. God wants us to eat correctly.

NUTRITIONAL CONVERSION

Before we begin to revamp our eating habits, we should have a "conversion" experience. We must become convicted that we have been eating incorrectly. We need to make a drastic change in the attitudes that have been deeply ingrained since childhood. As with every area of life, Christ is the only one who can give us both the desire and the power to change our appetites. Until we are willing to let Christ have control of this area, until we are converted to nutritious eating, we will never be able to change.

Several years ago a friend, Terri Nanney, shared with me about the improved health she had experienced through proper nutrition. I examined our family's eating habits. For years I thought that I had been preparing nutritious meals, only to discover that I had fallen into poor nutritional habits without even realizing it.

Deceitful Dainties versus Nutritious Nibblers

I found out that many of my snack foods were devoid of nutritional value. Out of my ignorance they had become a regular part of my daily fare. My grocery list included:

- Regular and diet cold drinks
- Cookies
- Crackers
- Pop tarts
- Sweet rolls and donuts
- Little chocolate cakes with pink icing

These modern nutritional disasters could probably be classified with what the Bible calls "deceitful dainties." Instead of these we can make available to our families some of many nutritious nibblers. The following are delicious:

- Unsalted mixed nuts
- Fresh fruit
- Dried fruit
- Carrot and celery sticks
- Peanut butter and honey
- Whole wheat bread
- Nutritious cookies
- Bran or carrot muffins
- Pumpkin, banana, or zucchini bread

Refined Foods

One of the chief causes of American nutritional robbery is the refining process. Refined products include white sugar, white flour, white rice, and common table salt. For many years I ignorantly thought I needed these products. I've learned through study that I don't need refined foods at all. Every nutrient and food I need can be supplied through natural sources.

Refined foods provide empty calories. Vitamins, trace minerals, and fiber have been removed. There is a difference between the life-giving natural carbohydrates and the death-giving, man-refined carbohydrates. A diet filled with fresh vegetables and fruits, dairy products, lean meat, legumes, natural oil, and whole grains is what God intended us to eat.

How to Get Started

I started the wrong way. Overnight I threw out all of the junk food in the house. I wouldn't recommend this unless you live by yourself and are very disciplined. It will be easier on your family if you work into this new way of eating gradually.

With a transition to good eating in mind, I therefore encourage three levels of nutritional changes covering foods to cut out, foods to cut down on, and foods to add to your diet.

Level One

Cut Out:

- Animal fat (fat of beef, sheep, and goats)
- Pork

Cut Down:

- Carbonated and caffeinated drinks
- Fried foods and snacks (chips, french fries, etc.)
- Desserts made with white sugar, white flour, and hydrogenated shortening
- Sugary snacks between meals
- Amount of meat eaten (no more than three to four ounces once a day)
- Amount of salad dressing (not more than one tablespoon per salad serving)
- Sugar-laden cereals and pastries
- Use of hydrogenated shortening and margarine

Add On:

- Six to eight glasses of water each day
- Whole grain or multigrain bread and cereals

- Brown rice
- Olive oil instead of other oils for stir-fry, salad dressings, etc.
- Stir-fry vegetables (in olive oil with small amount of meat)
- Have fresh fruit available for snacks at all times
- More raw-vegetable salads

LEVEL TWO

Cut Out:

- Foods with preservatives

Cut Down:

- Seafood scavengers (shrimp, crab, lobster, catfish, etc.)
- Red meat (no more than once a week)
- Amount of meat (Cut down on eating single-portion sizes and chop into small pieces for casseroles and stir-fry.)
- Carbonated and caffeinated drinks

Add On:

- Butter (sparingly) instead of margarine
- Pancakes, muffins, and pastries with whole-grain flour
- Oatmeal for cereal (Sprinkle with fresh fruit, raisins, nuts, or seeds.)
- Dried beans at least twice a week (navy beans, black beans, black-eyed peas, lentils, etc.)
- Plain yogurt (Make it yourself or choose a store brand without thickeners.)
- Fish at least once a week

LEVEL THREE

Cut Out:

- Seafood scavengers (shrimp, crab, lobster, catfish)
- Meat that contains antibiotics and growth hormones
- Red meat unless the blood has been drawn out (soak in water one-half hour, sprinkle with kosher salt, rinse, then broil)
- Cereals, snacks, and desserts made with white sugar and white flour (except on rare occasions)
- Carbonated sodas and caffeinated drinks (except on rare occasions)

Cut Down:

- Amount of meat (three to four ounces three or four times a week)

Add On:

- Home-ground whole grains
- Soy products as an alternative protein, i.e., tofu, veggie burgers, soy nuts, and soy milk
- Freshly juiced vegetables and fruit
- Add on more raw vegetables and fruit
- Homemade yogurt

I realize there are many controversial opinions about nutrition. I don't claim to be an expert, and I have written briefly about a complex topic. Some resource books on which I have based my conclusions are listed in the bibliography. As in all areas of life, I recommend that you examine various opinions, and then choose for yourself.

PART FOUR

Wisely Ministering

14

Women in Ministry

She extends her hand to the poor,
Yes, she reaches out her hands to the needy.

PROVERBS 31:20

A volatile question these days is: Has God called women into the ministry? I believe with all my heart that Jesus has called women to minister. Don't misunderstand—I didn't say to be pastors or overseers of the church, but to minister, to serve our Lord.

Perhaps this experience will help define what I mean by service. Several years ago my son David served overseas with the mission organization Operation Mobilization. He was part of the crew of one of their gospel ships called the *Doulos*. (*Doulos* is a Greek word meaning "servant.")

On January 1 Adrian and I met David in West Germany where the ship was docked. We stayed for several days as guests on board. Over three hundred young people and adults from forty countries were giving one, two, or more years of their lives, living sacrificially to share the good news of Jesus Christ.

Not only did they share their faith, but they cooked, cleaned, painted, repaired, sang, and prayed. When they docked, they went into prisons, old folks' homes, businessmen's luncheons, women's Bible studies, churches, and wherever else they could help distribute Christian literature and share their faith.

In those days I was challenged once again to minister—as I watched these young servants in action. And I was reminded that Jesus called everyone who loves Him to minister—men and women, young and old, rich and poor. But here I want to emphasize that Jesus indeed called women to minister to and for Him.

In this chapter I would like to introduce to you several women from the New Testament and from subsequent history who have used their talents and gifts to influence their world for Christ. In particular, I would like to honor six modern-day committed Christian women who have had a profound influence on my own life and on ministry to women.

These women have challenged me to keep my priorities as a wife and mother straight, to develop my own gifts, and, in God's proper timing, to channel my gifts to bless others. The women are from different parts of God's vineyard, and they have greatly encouraged other women to be surrendered to Christ and to employ their influence for His glory.

WOMEN WHOSE MINISTRIES HAVE CHALLENGED ME

VONETTE BRIGHT first gave me a vision of reaching women for Christ. The wife of Bill Bright, founder of Campus Crusade for Christ, she has motivated thousands of women to help change the conditions of the world through prayer and sharing their faith in the Lord, using the booklet *The Four Spiritual Laws.*

She is a role model of a wife who is a suitable helper to her husband, complementing him and not competing with him. She has developed her own gifts and ministry after fulfilling her priority assignment to her husband and then to her family.

She has had a worldwide impact through a special emphasis on prayer. She is the founder of The Great Commission Prayer Crusade of Campus Crusade. Several years ago she was the cochairman with Pat Boone of The National Day of Prayer, set aside by the president of the United States to pray for the leaders of our nation and the welfare of America. In 1984 she chaired The International Prayer Assembly in Seoul, Korea, which gathered three thousand international Christians dedicated to pray for the world. Her story is featured in the book *In Times Like These.*

JILL RENICH MYERS challenged me to reach out to meet the everyday needs of women that they might in turn reach out to others. She is the granddaughter of R. A. Torrey and the daughter of missionary parents. After being widowed, she is now married to Amos Myers, a preacher of the Gospel.

She founded the organization "Winning Women" in 1951. Winning

Women majors on meeting the needs of women as women, particularly through a biennial retreat ministry. These retreats have grown from fifty-seven to three thousand in attendance and from one location to numerous locations all over the nation. The sessions feature main speakers and a number of seminars to meet a woman's particular needs. Emphasis is especially placed on the areas of home life, Bible study, prayer, and helping women experience the reality of Christ's influence.

Jill has authored a number of books related to the home, including *To Have and to Hold*, translated into several languages, and *Between Us Women*.

JILL BRISCOE by example helped me "give up my right to myself" that I might be released to a larger place of living and ministry. Wife of Stuart Briscoe (pastor, author, and Bible conference leader), she is a dynamic Bible teacher, author, and women's conference speaker. As a young woman, she was motivated to "give up her rights" when Stuart was gone ten months of the year in a Bible-teaching ministry. During those lonely years she stepped out into unusual adventures of faith.

God used those experiences to speak through her to other women going through times of trial. Her husband was then called to the pastorate where she has established a tremendous Bible study and conference ministry to women. Now that her children are grown, she and Stuart frequently travel and speak together in the United States and abroad.

Her books include *Prime Rib and Apple, Queen of Hearts, A Time for Living*, and *Here Am I, Send Aaron*.

BEVERLY LAHAYE helped give me a burden for the family and for sharing the moral concerns of our day and then becoming involved. She is the wife of Tim LaHaye, who for years was a pastor, author, and conductor of family life seminars. In 1979 Beverly stepped out in faith and organized Concerned Women of America, which has grown to a membership of more than half a million. She has encouraged Christian women to pray and to become involved in moral concerns that deeply affect our families and our nation.

She has forthrightly exposed feminism and actively worked against the passage of the ERA. She has also worked against the forces of secular humanism. She has urged CWA supporters to give monetary aid for legal defense to Christians fighting court battles against humanism in the public schools and against legalized abortion.

Her books include *The Spirit-controlled Woman, How to Develop Your Child's Temperament*, and *Who But a Woman?*

ELISABETH ELLIOT, now Mrs. Lars Gren, stirred my soul to share the biblical role of women and to live a surrendered life. She has been widowed twice, being first married to Jim Elliot, one of five missionaries martyred by the Auca Indians in Ecuador. Elisabeth won the hearts of the Aucas and all of Christendom as she and her five-year-old daughter Valerie lived among the Aucas and exhibited to them the love and forgiveness of Christ.

Radio listeners can hear Elisabeth each day on her program "Gateway to Joy," where she invites women to consider their roles and responsibilities in light of biblical principles. Elisabeth offers a scholarly approach to the biblical roles of men and women and challenges them to live sacrificially for Christ and to maintain purity before marriage, and fidelity afterward. In her dynamic speaking she lifts up the role of the homemaker to this generation of women.

She has become a renowned author. Her books include *Shadow of the Almighty, Passion and Purity, Through Gates of Splendor, Let Me Be a Woman, No Graven Image, Discipline: The Glad Surrender,* and *Love Has a Price Tag.*

DAISY HEPBURN motivated me to combine spiritual life and moral concerns in a ministry to women. Wife of David Hepburn, director of ministries at Missions Springs Conference Center in Northern California, she is a powerful speaker and motivator of women. Conferences, conventions, women's retreats, radio, and television have carried her messages across the continent.

She is the founder of Hope of our Heritage conferences, which have had an impact on evangelical Christian women all across the nation. She has also been instrumental in helping churches grow effective women's ministries through stressing a creative and balanced program of spiritual growth and outreach. She is the author of the Life with Spice programs and the books *Why Doesn't Somebody Do Something?* and *Lead, Follow, or Get Out of the Way.*

NEW TESTAMENT EXAMPLES

Don't just believe me when I say God can and does use women. Don't even believe simply because I can list off the names of six modern-day women who are experiencing fruitful ministries for Christ. Don't even believe because of the missionaries (men and women) I observed on the *Doulos.* God's Word is replete with examples of women whose ministry God honored with His hand of blessing. In particular, think of these New Testament women:

• Jesus chose to come into this world through a woman's womb, the womb of a virgin named Mary. We see her ministering to Jesus from the day she gave birth in the stable in Bethlehem to the day she stood at the foot of His cross in Jerusalem, and even beyond.

• It was a hated Samaritan woman to whom Jesus spoke at the well and offered a drink of living water—and that at a time when men didn't speak to women in public, especially to women of her race and reputation. It was this woman who hurriedly abandoned her water pot and ran back into the city, proclaiming to the men, "Come see a man, who told me everything I ever did: is this not the Christ?"

• At the foot of Jesus' cross, when most of the disciples already had fled, fearing for their safety—the Bible says in Matthew 27:55 that "many women who followed Jesus from Galilee, ministering to Him, were there looking on from afar."

• Several women (including Mary Magdalene) were first at the empty tomb. And the angel commanded them to, "Go quickly and tell His disciples that He is risen from the dead." God chose women as the first to tell the good news of Jesus' resurrection.

• Women were among those obeying Jesus by waiting with the disciples in the upper room for the "promise of the Father" (Acts 1).

• It was a woman—Lydia, a seller of purple—who opened her home and said to the apostle Paul in Acts 16:15, "If you have judged me to be faithful to the Lord, come to my house and stay."

• It was a woman—Priscilla—who helped her husband instruct Apollos, an eloquent man mighty in the Scriptures (see Acts 18:24).

• And it was a woman—Phoebe—about whom Paul said in Romans 16:1, "I commend to you Phoebe our sister, who is a servant of the church in Cenchrea."

OTHER WOMEN IN HISTORY AND TODAY

LOTTIE MOON was the first fully appointed woman missionary of the Foreign Mission Board of the Southern Baptist Convention in 1873. Her example stimulated the development of women's missionary societies. Miss Moon proposed an offering at Christmastime in order to send new women missionaries to relieve her in China, where she had worked without furlough, often alone, for eleven years. Thus the Lottie Moon Christmas offering was named in her honor.[1]

ANNIE ARMSTRONG was the founder and the first corresponding secretary of the Woman's Missionary Union of the Southern Baptist Convention in 1888. She is described as a "sharp, forceful, tall, attractive, second generation women's leader, for six years the foremost female advocate for home missions."[2] Her genius was bringing forces together, an ability she recognized as God-given. However, she understood Paul's biblical writings in the most literal sense: She refused to speak to mixed groups of men and women.[3]

BETTY STAM, along with her husband John, was a missionary to China, sent out by the China Inland Mission—she in 1931 and he in 1932. Married a year later, they labored courageously and were martyred by the Chinese Communists in 1934. Betty and John displayed an unshakable trust in God.

Thirty hours after their death their three-month-old daughter, Helen Priscilla, was discovered in a deserted house by a traveling Christian, Evangelist Lo. "He found her lying on the bed, just as her mother's hands and heart had planned. Safe in her sleeping bag with its zipper fastened, little Helen was warm and snug, and seemingly none the worse for her long fast. Inside the sleeping bag Betty had tucked away a clean nightdress and some diapers, all she had been able to bring with her, and among them she had pinned two five-dollar bills."[4] Betty Stam's parents wrote, "God could no less surely have saved the lives of her precious parents had that been in His divine plan for them."

BERTHA SMITH was over one hundred years old when she died. "Miss Bertha," as she was lovingly called, was appointed by the Foreign Mission Board of the Southern Baptist Convention in 1917. She served in China beginning in 1919 and was there during the great Shantung revival. In 1948 the Communists forced her to leave, and she was transferred to Taiwan as the first missionary of the SBC Foreign Mission Board on that island. After her retirement "Miss Bertha" traveled and spoke throughout our land and had a profound influence on the lives of multitudes, including my husband and me.

CORRIE TEN BOOM, who died in the United States at age ninety, served time in a German concentration camp during World War II for the crime of hiding persecuted Jews. She was sustained by her great faith. Self-styled "tramp for the Lord," she tirelessly traveled all over the globe for thirty years sharing the reality of Jesus Christ. Her dynamic story is told in her book *The Hiding Place* and portrayed on film under the same title. She won the hearts of the American Christians through sharing her testimony in Billy Graham Crusades and in numerous books.

MARY SLESSOR sailed for Nigeria in 1876 and worked there until her death. She fought against witchcraft, drunkenness, twin-killing, and other cruel customs. She believed in "the daily mixing with the people" to break down suspicion and fear. She was fluent in local languages and had an almost uncanny insight into the African mind. She had an unusual combination of qualities—humor and seriousness, roughness and tenderness, vision and practicality. These, with a cool nerve and disregard for personal health and comfort, helped to make her a powerful influence for Christianity. As a result of her work under God, the Ibo people became more committed Christians than people in other parts of Nigeria.

HENRIETTA MEARS was the inspiration and genius of the great Sunday school of the First Presbyterian Church of Hollywood, California, with its six thousand members. In that Sunday school she taught the now-famous college class, in addition to administering the school. She was the founder of Gospel Light Publications, which still publishes conservative literature and books.[5] She also saw her vision of a Bible conference center at Forest Home come into reality. There many outstanding Christian leaders were influenced for Christ, including Bill and Vonette Bright. Her book, *What the Bible Is All About,* has had over 1,250,000 copies in print and has pointed multitudes to see Jesus in every book of the Bible. This book and the story of Miss Mears's life has had a profound impact on my own life.

These are but a smattering of the multitudes of godly women, servants of their Lord, many of whose names are known to God alone. In fact, all who know and love Jesus Christ are called to be servants, to minister for their Lord.

15

Ministering Under Authority

Therefore, my beloved brethren, be steadfast, immovable,
always abounding in the work of the Lord,
knowing that your labor is not in vain in the Lord.

1 CORINTHIANS 15:58

There's a strong movement today to show that women are as intelligent and gifted as men and that a woman can do any job a man can do. But the issue isn't inferiority or superiority. Jesus set straight once for all the misconception caused by sin that women were inferior.

Yes, down through history women have been abused, enslaved, and treated like property. Sin causes the man to physically and mentally abuse the woman, and sin also causes the woman to manipulate and misuse the man. Jesus came to deliver both the man and the woman, who are of equal worth. The apostle Paul declares it in Galatians 3:28: "There is neither Jew nor Greek, there is neither slave nor free, there is neither male nor female; for you are all one in Christ Jesus."

But nowhere did God declare a sameness of roles. There are individual tasks that can be done by either a man or a woman according to who is better gifted. For instance, a man or a woman can mow the lawn, cut hair, take out the garbage, keep the checkbook, etc. Many of these tasks have been assigned by custom, not by Scripture. And frankly, I'm going to stick with the custom of the man mowing the lawn, although I know some women who enjoy this task. If they want to do it, that's fine with me. However, we must learn to discern between custom and the principles of God's Word.

I recently read the story of a Christian woman's struggle with the feeling that her work wasn't considered as important as the work of a man. She had the feeling that women, even in the Christian world, were given "second-class" status. From this feeling she presents the premise that the curse of the Fall has been lifted and that women have been restored to co-dominion in God's order. She believes, however, that in the home the woman is still to be in submission to her husband, but in "God's kingdom" they are to have "balanced authority." She is a co-pastor with her husband.

I suggest that this lovely lady, sincere as she is, has reached a wrong conclusion through faulty reasoning. First of all, it was Satan who suggested to her that her work wasn't as important as the work of a man. A woman's work certainly is as important as a man's work. It is just different. Besides, if she assumes that the work traditionally called women's work is not as important as the man's, then she is suggesting that whoever does that work has a less important job, for someone will have to do those jobs—either a man or a woman.

I have had help from time to time to make my workload easier. But I don't believe the household servant I have employed to help me is inferior. I do not want to give her jobs that are demeaning to her. Cleaning toilets and ironing the clothes may not be my favorite thing to do, but I never feel inferior when I do these things. The Bible says, "And whatever you do, do all to the glory of God" (Col. 3:17). Secondly, if indeed God had "lifted the curse" and granted co-dominion or equal leadership, I believe it would have applied to the home as well. I do believe that the curse of the Fall has been lifted, but the curse was spiritual death. Praise God, through Jesus' death on the cross I have been set free from the curse of sin and death.

I believe some consequences to Adam and Eve's sin still remain. There are still weeds and thorns in the ground and pain in childbirth. God allowed these consequences to remain. From other Scriptures in the New Testament we have already studied, we find that God still has placed the woman under man's headship. It is for her protection—for her good.

My husband had an associate pastor whose name is Bob Sorrell. Bob was under the authority of my husband. But Bob was God's gift to my husband—to come alongside him, to help, to advise, to gently remind, to help evaluate and organize the many facets of our church. That Bob was not the pastor of our church didn't make his function any less important. In fact, our church is so large that my husband could not have pastored the people without Bob's valuable help.

Bob knew my husband's heart. He was loyal, diligent, and trustworthy. He had much influence on my husband and thus on the ministry of our church. My husband delegated to Bob vast areas of responsibility. But Bob kept in touch with my husband to make sure that his actions were in keeping with my husband's desires. Since he was under authority, he had been delegated authority in large areas of our church administration.

EXAMINING THE SCRIPTURE

Everywhere we go, someone is in charge. God allows us to use our creativity and to develop the details in all areas of our lives. But there are foundational lines of authority in the Bible for the ministry of women. The woman is encouraged—yes, commanded to minister—to serve. But she is not to take authority over the man. She is to minister under authority. Where does it say that? In God's Word. Let's examine two major passages on this subject.

> *Let the woman quietly receive instruction with entire submissiveness. But I do not allow a woman to teach or exercise authority over a man, but to remain quiet. (1 Tim. 2:11-12 NASB).*

In the sphere of doctrinal disputes or questions of interpretation, where authoritative pronouncements are to be made, the woman is to keep silence. Also in a position of ruling or authority over men, the woman is to remain quiet. If she has questions, the Bible says she is to ask her husband at home. She is not to be the official teacher or doctrine setter of the church.

Some say that this was just the custom of the day. Granted, some issues may relate to custom, but Paul does not appeal to custom. He goes as far back as the Garden of Eden for his explanation. Others say Paul was prejudiced against women because of his rabbinical training. This view about Paul implies, however, that some parts of the Bible are the word of man—not the Word of God. We do know that the entire Bible is the Word of God.

What did Paul say? Two simple statements from 1 Timothy 2:

1. Verse 13—"For Adam was formed first, then Eve." Adam was put in charge by virtue of the order of creation. We read in 1 Corinthians 11:8-9, "For man is not from woman, but woman from man. Nor was man created for the woman, but woman for the man." That was God's original idea. Paul goes on to say in verses 11 and 12, "Nevertheless, neither is man independent of woman, nor woman independent of man, in the Lord. For as

woman came from man, even so man also comes through woman; but all things are from God."

Yes, the man is in charge, but he is not to minister or carry on without the woman's help. She was made to be a suitable helper. He needs her advice and insights. Yes, some men say by their actions, "I'll do it all by myself." But God says, "Don't forget to listen to the helper I gave you." I believe the classic example of a man who should have listened to the advice of his helper was Pontius Pilate.

2. Verse 14—"And Adam was not deceived, but the woman being deceived, fell into transgression." It may have been all the woman's fault, or perhaps Adam failed in his responsibility. Yes, the woman was the first to sin. But the Bible says, "Therefore, just as through one man sin entered the world, and death through sin, and thus death spread to all men, because all sinned"(Rom. 5:12). First Corinthians 15:22 says, "As in Adam [not Eve] all die. . . ."

Adam was Eve's supervisor. She was deceived, but he was over her, and he had to take full responsibility for her actions. If Adam wasn't deceived, he sinned with his eyes wide open. There has been a lot of speculation about this. Some say that Adam loved Eve so much that he couldn't bear to be without her, so he willingly sinned.

A Second Scripture

Let your women keep silent in the churches, for they are not permitted to speak; but they are to be submissive, as the law also says. And if they want to learn something, let them ask their own husbands at home; for it is shameful for women to speak in church. (1 Cor. 14:34-35)

The word *silent* can be translated "quietness." This doesn't necessarily mean that a woman cannot say a word, but that she shouldn't be bossy, wanting to take control. She should have a meek and quiet spirit.

Paul says in 1 Corinthians 11:5, 13-15 that a woman may pray or prophesy if she has her head covered. What the literal head covering was has been debated by godly people down through the ages. Some say it was a veil or hat. Others say it is long hair. Still others say that it is hair long enough and in an appropriate style to show the difference between the man and the woman. It may have been a custom, and customs may change. But regardless of how you interpret it, the meaning does not change. I believe the meaning behind the symbol is clear—it shows a woman's willingness to be under authority.

PROPER PRIORITY

Ministry is not limited to activities in and through the church, so none of us is ever exempt from ministry. But the sphere and the extent of your ministry depends upon the proper priority in your life.

God's Word makes it plain in 1 Corinthians 7:34 that the single woman and the married woman have a different set of priorities. The woman who is called by God to a life of singleness can have a unique relationship to her Lord. The central focus of her life can be to please her Lord (see 1 Cor. 7:32). There will be more time to be alone with God, more time for sharing with others about Jesus, and more time for ministering to those who are suffering. But everyone is not called to this kind of life. Paul says, "every man hath his proper gift of God." Obviously, the single life, even of service, is not meant for everyone, or there would not be a human race. God has called some special people to be single for the kingdom of God (see Matt. 19:12).

I know some of you are single parents and out of necessity must leave your children with others to provide the necessities of life. My hat is off to you, and my blessings are upon you! If you must work, there are multitudes of opportunities for you to minister day by day.

If, however, you are a married woman, be careful not to neglect your God-assigned priorities. Don't try to enjoy the benefits of marriage and family without the priorities attached. What are some factors in determining the sphere and extent of a married woman's ministry? Are you fulfilling God's chief assignment as stated in Titus 2:5 to be "homemakers"? Let me give you a little quiz to see if you are.

- What are the desires of your husband?
- Do you keep your home clean and attractive?
- Do you provide nutritious meals in a relaxed atmosphere?
- Do you keep your family attractively and neatly clothed?
- Do you take time to be a thrifty shopper?
- Do you keep yourself rested so you can have a meek and quiet spirit?
- Are you hospitable to family and friends, reaching out to those in physical and spiritual need?
- Do you take time to train your children and be involved in their activities?
- Do you make time to keep yourself attractive and interesting—being an encourager and a lover to your husband?

• Do you strive to excel instead of just getting by at being a wife, mother, and homemaker?

These responsibilities, whose order may vary depending upon your stage of life, comprise your chief assignment from God. When you have fulfilled this assignment, you may then extend the sphere of your ministry in consultation with your husband and in communion with God.

THE PRACTICE OF A WOMAN'S MINISTRY

I want to give six examples of New Testament women for you to follow as you seek to minister for the Lord under authority.

Work at Being Winsome with the Woman at the Well

> *The woman then left her waterpot, went her way into the city, and said to the men, "Come, see a Man who told me all things that I ever did. Could this be the Christ?" (John 4:28-29)*

This woman went back to those she knew and told what she had seen and heard. We must note, however, that she had experienced a change in her life and that her experience with the Lord had power to draw people to Christ. Notice that it didn't say she told the women but that she told the men about Jesus. She probably would not have been received by the women. But she went to whom she could with her life-changing message.

Someone is waiting to hear what God has done for you. Go first to those who know you best—to your family, your friends, to the people with whom you work. Go first even to those with whom you've sinned. Some will see and respond to the changed life they witness. If they will not receive the message of life, then tell it to whoever will listen. Talk about Christ to your beautician, your dentist, the bag boy at the grocery store. Tell it on your job, in the classroom, at the PTA meeting. Win some with the woman at the well.

Learn a Lesson from Lydia

> *And on the Sabbath day we went out of the city to the riverside, where prayer was customarily made; and we sat down and spoke to the women who met there. Now a certain woman named Lydia heard us. She was a seller of purple from the city of Thyatira, who worshiped God. The Lord opened her heart to heed the things spoken by Paul. And when she and her household were baptized, she begged us, saying, "If you have judged me to be faithful to the Lord, come to my house and stay." So she persuaded us. (Acts 16:13-15)*

Lydia used her home to serve her Lord. She invited Paul to stay at her house and shared her provisions with him. What a blessing comes to those who will open their hearts and homes to God's servants. There is no better way to influence your children for godliness than to have in your home people who are servants of God.

Besides offering hospitality to God's servants, there are a variety of ways to open your home as a witness for Christ. Start in your neighborhood. A good way to reach out to the women in your neighborhood is to have a neighborhood evangelistic tea. Prepare refreshments and beautiful flowers and invite your neighbors over. You can invite a friend to share her testimony of what Christ means in her life. There are various ways of sharing Christ so as not to be offensive. Another possibility is to have a backyard Bible club for the children in your neighborhood. Always be sure to be up front with what you are doing.

Discern What Dorcas Did

> At Joppa there was a certain disciple named Tabitha, which is translated Dorcas. This woman was full of good works and charitable deeds which she did. . . .Then Peter arose and went with them. When he had come, they brought him to the upper room. And all the widows stood by him weeping, showing the tunics and garments which Dorcas had made while she was with them. (Acts 9:26, 29)

Dorcas was an able seamstress who used her creativity to minister to others. In Bellevue Baptist Church a sewing group meets every week to sew stuffed animals for the children in the pediatric wing of Baptist Hospital in Memphis. They also sew little carriers in the shapes of valentines for those babies who go home on Valentine's Day.

With these gifts made by loving hands is given a New Testament and a little book. These are meant to be a witness for our Lord. Few people visit the sewing room, but God meets with them on Tuesdays. He knows, and He blesses these "cups of cold water" given in His name.

Perhaps you can't sew. Can you bake bread? Then take a freshly baked loaf to that neighbor and tell her about Jesus, the Bread of Life. Do you grow beautiful flowers? Take a bouquet to a sick friend and share with her about Jesus, the Rose of Sharon. Can you write a poem or sing a song? Use that talent to minister to someone who is lonely or sad.

I remember some years ago when my daughter Janice was pregnant with her first child and was sick a good deal of the time. She took up cross-stitching to ease the misery. The husband of a good friend died, and Janice had the idea of cross-stitching the Bible verse, "Weeping may endure for a night, but joy comes in the morning" (Ps. 30:56). She said, "Mother, if you will pay for the frame, I will do the stitching." Mary Hunter was so blessed and touched by this gift from her young friend that they developed a closeness that continued many years.

Pursue Priscilla's Plan

> *So he began to speak boldly in the synagogue. When Aquila and Priscilla heard him, they took him aside and explained to him the way of God more accurately. (Acts 18:26)*

Priscilla was a helper to her husband. She joined with Aquila to help Apollos understand God's ways. Many times as I've been along when my husband visited the hospital or a home, God has given me just the right word of encouragement or comfort. On occasion when we've been standing around a bedside at a crisis hour, Adrian has asked me to sing a song. A favorite request of his is a simple Scripture song: "They that trust in the Lord shall be as Mount Zion, which cannot be removed, but abideth forever. As the mountains are round about Jerusalem, so the Lord is round about his people from this time forth and forever" (Ps. 125:1-2 KJV).

If your husband is also a Christian, you can share hospitality together. One Christmas we were living in a new neighborhood in a new city. No one on our street knew who we were. We decided to have a neighborhood open house. We sent out invitations and at the bottom wrote these words: "We will share the true meaning of Christmas." At a good point in the evening, we gathered in the living room around the piano and sang Christmas carols. A friend sang a couple of Christmas songs, and my husband shared brief thoughts about what Christmas meant to us. The Lord used us in that neighborhood to reach out while we lived there.

Our church provides many opportunities to be involved in sharing the Gospel in other parts of the United States and overseas, as well as in our own city. I have had the privilege on a number of occasions to go with my husband and share in this ministry—singing, giving a testimony, praying, and visiting in the homes with national (local) Christians. It has been one of the highlights of my life to visit such countries as Brazil, Argentina, Korea, S. Africa, Honduras, Russia, and Romania.

Emulate Eunice's Example

When I call to remembrance the genuine faith that is in you, which dwelt first in your grandmother Lois and your mother Eunice, and I am persuaded is in you also. (2 Tim. 1:5)

Eunice influenced young Timothy by her life of genuine faith. Don't let someone else have the joy of leading your children to Christ. How wonderful it has been to teach my children and to know that partly through my influence they came to know the Lord.

I now have the joy of seeing this faith multiplied as I see my children teaching their children the things of the Lord. Walking along the beach, I've sung to my grandchildren the same song I sang to my children, "Oh, who can make the seashells? I'm sure I can't—can you? No one can make the seashells. No one but God, 'tis true!"

A number of years ago I experienced one of the greatest joys of my life. We made a special trip to Florida to witness the baptism of our first grandchild, Renae. What a thrill for Grammy to be able to take video pictures as her granddaddy put her under the baptismal waters. I gave her a special Jerusalem cross that I had purchased in the Holy Land to remember that significant occasion. Other grandchildren have now followed in believers' baptism, to outwardly demonstrate the inward reality of faith in Christ.

Follow the Faith of Phoebe

I commend to you Phoebe our sister, who is a servant of the church in Cenchrea, that you may receive her in the Lord in a manner worthy of the saints, and assist her in whatever business she has need of you; for indeed she has been a helper of many and of myself also. (Rom. 16:1)

Phoebe was a faithful servant of the church. She didn't have to be the pastor to be used of God. We as women can teach women and children in Sunday school, lead youth groups, work with the needy, serve in the women's ministry, invite the unsaved to church-wide events, serve on committees, decorate for luncheons or special events, arrange flowers, serve in the nursery, open our homes to entertain guests of the church, sing in the choir, and a multitude of other things. Whatever your circumstances, God has called you into His ministry. He just wants you to minister under authority and with the proper priority.

16

Building Bridges to the Community

Be hospitable to one another without grumbling.
As each one has received a gift, minister it to one another,
as good stewards of the manifold grace of God.

1 PETER 4:9-10

A wise woman builds bridges to others in her community, her nation, and her world. This is a significant portion of her ministry. As in all other areas of ministry, one of the chief means of building these bridges is through prayer. This is our avenue of communication and of dependence on our Lord; so let's take a few moments to contemplate prayer as we begin to assess our degree of influence in our communities and beyond.

APPROACHING GOD

As we approach prayer, it isn't the position of our bodies, but the attitude of our hearts that really matters. We must come to Him first with meekness. Jesus said, "Blessed are the meek; for they shall inherit the earth" (Matt. 5:5). This means our spirits will be submissive, easily guided and controlled by the Lord. The blessings of meekness run through the whole Bible.

Next we must know God's Word so we can know what to pray for. Over the years, God has shown me countless promises from His Word and invited me to apply them in relation to family, friends, and circumstances in my life. This knowledge released the faith to believe God for answered prayer. Jesus said, "If you abide in Me, and My words abide in you, you will ask what you desire, and it shall be done for you" (John 15:7).

Knowledge of God's Word is closely linked with obedience to His Word. If we are abiding in Jesus, we are obeying. Abiding means living in Him, being so related to Him that we know what He wants. If the previous concepts are true in our lives, then we only need ask in the name of Jesus for the things we desire, and we will receive them (John 16:23-24).

Finally we need a method of praying. The one I use is a five-point prayer plan. This includes confession, praise, thanksgiving, intercession, and petition.

Confession—"If we confess our sins, He is faithful and just to forgive us our sins, and to cleanse us from all unrighteousness" (1 John 1:9). Our hearts must be clean—all sins confessed. God won't pay attention when we pray if we harbor sin in our lives. "If I regard iniquity in my heart, the Lord will not hear" (Ps. 66:18).

Praise and Thanksgiving—"Enter into His gates with thanksgiving, and into His courts with praise. Be thankful to Him, and bless His name" (Ps. 100:4). It is impossible to separate these two kinds of prayer, but there is a difference. Praise is telling God how great He is and how much we love Him for who He is. (Some call this adoration or worship.) Thanksgiving is saying thank you for all He has done for us. Psalm 116:17 says we should offer to Him the sacrifice of thanksgiving. When we begin praising, we will continue thanking. When we are thankful, our hearts will burst forth in praise.

Intercession—"I exhort first of all that supplications, prayers, intercessions, and giving of thanks be made for all men" (1 Tim. 2:1). One of the greatest ministries is praying for others. Jesus is our great example. He is seated at the right hand of His Father, interceding for us (Heb. 7:25). Anyone may participate in this ministry. Everyone should. Some are shut-in and bedridden, thinking their lives are useless. The high calling of intercessory prayer is still open to them. A special notebook is helpful for this ministry.

Petition—"Give us this day our daily bread" (Matt. 6:11). Finally we come asking for ourselves. I have listed it last on purpose. We should pray for ourselves many times a day. If the rest of our prayer lives are in order, this part will be too. We won't always be praying "gimme" prayers. We will be praying, "Not my will, but Yours be done."

Solomon received the privilege of asking God for anything he wanted. He prayed unselfishly. He asked for wisdom to judge his people. I want my chief prayer to be for me to be filled with the wisdom of God. If this is my desire, God has promised to answer my petition. "If any of you lacks wisdom, let him ask of God, who gives to all liberally and without reproach, and it will be given to him" (James 1:5).

BUILDING BRIDGES THROUGH OUTREACH

Those who are wise shall shine like the brightness of the firmament, and those who turn many to righteousness like the stars forever and ever. (Dan. 12:3)

A woman should not isolate herself from others just because her priority is her home. Her primary field of outreach is her home. However, she will reach out and touch those beyond it. Even when children are small and time and energy limited, there are creative ways of ministering to others and bringing joy to the world.

Encouraging Words

The telephone can be a blessing or a curse. With it you can encourage and comfort, or you can gossip and tear down. You can even pray with someone on the phone. I have done it many times.

Cards and notes of comfort and cheer can be sent to the sick and bereaved. Don't forget to send a word to rejoice with those with new babies, a promotion, or a special recognition.

Short Visits

As you step outside your door, walk into your neighborhood with the good news about Jesus. Start with a short friendly visit and a warm loaf of homemade bread or a pot of homemade soup, especially to greet newcomers on the block.

Some memorable occasions for me have been neighborhood Christmas parties centered around Christ. One year I hosted a ladies' neighborhood coffee. We had lovely Christmas goodies and sang Christmas carols. Then I shared the true meaning of Christmas. Another time we had a family open house. My children didn't think anyone would come, but the whole house was full of men, women, and children from our neighborhood.

Why not try a "Love Thy Neighbor" coffee at Valentine's Day or a "Celebrate the Wonder of Springtime" tea when the flowers are growing in profusion? Better yet, why not call your neighbor on the phone right now and ask her to come over for a cup of apple cider or hot tea?

My friend Barbara Ball said that she made a habit of just being "chatty for Jesus." If you begin a friendly conversation, it may develop into an occasion to share about Christ. If not, it didn't hurt to be nice.

The Written Word

I usually carry several different kinds of tracts in case I want to give one to the bag carrier at the grocery store, the service station attendant, or the waitress at a restaurant (with a tip).

Christian books also are a wonderful means of encouragement and witness. There are hundreds of suitable paperback books as well as others that will uniquely meet someone's need.

Just Visiting

Planned visitation is, of course, greatly used by the Lord. In my lifetime I've visited in homes for the elderly, the hospital, children's homes, jails, and private residences. Years ago when my house was filled with small children, I bordered on feeling sorry for myself because I had so much to do.

During my Sunday school class visitation, I knocked on the door of a seventeen-year-old mother with a hydrocephalic baby. Then I visited in a home for the elderly, and people were just sitting around with nothing to do. I still remember praising God all the way home for my household of healthy children and for so much work to do.

Church-based Opportunities

I have always been involved in my local church—even before I was a preacher's wife. There are many opportunities to minister through the church. I have taught children, teenagers, and adults. I love them all. For years I have taught a class for children who are new Christians. They are such a joy. And just think, they have their whole lives to give in service for Jesus.

I've heard and studied about missions all my life. I have prayed for others who want to be missionaries and given my money so they could go. But one of the highlights of my life was when my husband and I went with a group of laypeople from our church to Taiwan, the Republic of China, to share Christ.

What a blessing to experience for myself the oneness in Christ between us and the Chinese Christians there. We were only there for a week, but when we left, I loved them so much. We went door to door witnessing with the Chinese Christians. In my own strength this type of witnessing is the hardest of all, but I felt His strength.

I have helped plan evangelistic outreach projects for women through my church. The women of the church invite a friend, neighbor, or acquaintance with a spiritual need. A creative theme is chosen, lovely decorations made, delicious food served, and beautiful music presented. All of this points toward the time of sharing Christ. (An outstanding Christian woman should be invited to speak about the difference Christ makes in a woman's world.) Of course, the occasion affords an opportunity to begin or continue a witnessing relationship with the one brought to the luncheon.

These are but a few of the countless ways we women can extend Christ's influence into our communities. Be creative. Express your unique personality. God will provide the planks as you faithfully work to build His bridges into your world.

JOY TO THE WORLD

THE WORLD NEEDS JOY!

> *The poor and hungry need this joy—*
> *The red and yellow,*
> *black and white,*
> *The lonely and sorrowing,*
> *The defeated and dejected,*
> *The immoral and the moral—*
> *They all need joy!*

THE WORLD IS LOOKING FOR JOY!

> *It looks here and there for joy.*
> *It looks in possessions*
> *and in pleasures.*
> *It looks in popularity*
> *and in power,*
> *But joy is never found*
> *in these!*

I HAVE FOUND A JOY!

> *A joy so deep within—*
> *A joy that lingers*
> *even when I'm sad*
> *and crying.*

I WANT TO SHARE MY JOY!

I want the world to
 know my joy so—

JOY TO THE WORLD!

THE JOY OF THE WORLD CAME
DOWN THAT FIRST CHRISTMAS!

It came in a humble way,
 yet heralded by angels.
It came to a little town,
 the little town of Bethlehem.

Hardly anyone knew that
 "Joy" came to the world
 that night long ago.
But here I am almost 2000
 years hence,
 and I know.

I KNOW THE JOY OF THE WORLD!

Because one told one,
 and two told two,
 and three told three.
Then someone told me that

JESUS IS THAT JOY!

Born so long ago,
Born to die upon a cross,
Born
 to take my sadness
 and my sin,
 to take my loneliness
 and guilt,
 to take my fear and doubt,
 to take my selfishness
 and hate.

SO TO THE WORLD SO LONG AGO
THE FATHER SENT HIS
"GREATEST JOY."

The Joy that shared the
Father's heart,
The Joy in whom all fullness
of the Godhead lived.

Jesus said,
"Exchange your sadness
and your weakness
for My joy,
For My joy shall be
your strength.
I came to flood your life
with joy
So full and overflowing
that you too must
share My joy
with those
around you—

Around your family circle,
Around the nearest block,
Around the town in which you live,
And then indeed
Around the world."

17

Trends, Pressures, and Hopes

Strength and honor are her clothing;
She shall rejoice in time to come.

PROVERBS 31:25

Feminism, I believe, is not synonymous with femininity or being ladylike. Feminism indicates a desire to be equal with men in their role or function, and it involves a resistance against commonly accepted traditional roles.

The secular feminist crusades for equal rights because she has not experienced the equality of worth one gains from being in Christ. Without spiritual perception she is not able to discern between God's established principles, man-made customs, and sin-related abuses, so she cannot arrive at the correct solution to her problems.

With a spirit of love for my sisters in Christ, I want us to deal with the problems of feminism. We will look at the secular feminists' position so that a Christian woman can be aware of this philosophy and make sure she is not unknowingly emulating this point of view in lesser ways.

The Christian woman should be aware that there are those who call themselves biblical feminists. They certainly do not fall into the category of the secular feminists. However, I would differ with biblical feminists in their outlook on the nature of holy Scripture and its interpretation.

We must recognize that there are varying degrees of this position, and that everyone claiming to be a biblical feminist may not agree with all of the positions of those on the far left of this approach. It is obvious, however, when scanning bibliographies on this subject, that the major resource material has come from more radical biblical feminists outside the ranks of conservative evangelicals in general. Most evangelical Christian women, and even many pastors, are not aware of the beliefs of the biblical feminists and where this philosophy could lead.

LEGITIMATE CONCERNS OF WOMEN *AND* MEN

I do not deny that there have been and are serious problems related to the treatment of women. Indeed, if there were no legitimate problems, there would be no extreme feminist movement. Down through the ages women have been taken advantage of, sexually abused, and even enslaved because of their lesser physical strength. Sometimes men feel threatened by strong-willed or intelligent women.

God originally designed the woman to be a highly esteemed helper or associate. In many cases she has been denied this position, and her duties have been limited to only menial tasks. Indeed, many a woman dreads the drudgery of washing, ironing, meal preparation, and the constant care of children with hardly a bathroom break. There is little appreciation for these thankless tasks, and at the end of most days, she is so tired she feels like falling into bed instead of being romantic.

The woman is so often caught up in the "myriad of the mundane" that she forgets to admire her man's accomplishments and to soothe his troubled brow. Men and women often forget the "dignity of drudgery" and that nothing worthwhile is gained without hours of routine—whether it's becoming a brain surgeon, a concert pianist, or raising godly children.

There are different degrees of problems related to the treatment of women. Some have been grievously abused—mentally and/or physically. They have been put down, knocked down, cursed, or neglected. Others have been mildly mistreated or simply ignored. Many women are starved for attention from a man who sits in front of the television or hides behind his newspaper night after night.

Often the woman has not been appreciated for her God-given abilities and insights but has been ridiculed for not behaving or thinking like a man. The woman may not realize it, but she may unconsciously be attempting to measure up to the qualities she sees the man admire. Perhaps he would not admit it, but his lack of appreciation for the woman's uniquely God-given qualities may have driven her to emulate the male-appreciated qualities.

The abuses and misuses of men and women are related to that little three-letter word *sin*. Right in the middle of that word is the key to our problem—the big I. Selfishness is a sin problem and is at the center of all male-female problems. But clamoring for equal rights is not the answer. I feel this demand only produces masculinized women. The softness of femininity has been rubbed off.

The only answer to the sin problem is Christ. Only as we lay our selfish rights at His feet are we able to rebuild right relationships with the opposite sex.

PRESSURES

Pressures have arisen from some feminists to eliminate the commonly accepted biblical interpretation of the woman's role in the home and in the church. One example of this is the National Organization for Women. In its official booklet called "Revolution: Tomorrow Is Now," the following resolution appears:

> In the light of the enslavement of body and mind which the church historically has imposed on women, we demand that the seminaries:
>
> a. Immediately stop and repudiate their propagation of sexist, male supremist doctrine,
>
> b. Initiate women's study courses which cut through the traditional male, religious mythology to expose church and other social forces denying women their basic human dignity,
>
> c. Actively recruit, employ, and justly promote women theologians and other staff in all departments,
>
> d. Actively recruit, enroll, financially aid, and seek equal placement for women theological students.[1]

Secular feminism does not look to God's Word and His wisdom to deal with the problems related to the treatment of women. Assuming to know what equality is, the feminist seeks to attain it by her own ingenuity. Thinking this means she should be able to work at any job a man can, she seeks to free herself of any encumbrances that would prevent her from attaining this goal.

This entails freeing herself from unwanted pregnancies and the daily so-called drudgery of childcare. Thus she may justify abortion. Aiming to succeed in the male-oriented workplace, she either postpones marriage and childbearing or decides not to pursue these tasks.

Sometimes those women who have been rejected, neglected, or abused by men turn to lesbian relationships in an attempt to find acceptance and tenderness. But failing to find her guidance from God's Word, she distorts God's purpose for her life, misusing even God-intended female friendships.

The extreme feminist is also a humanist. Tim LaHaye in his book *The Battle for the Mind* says that "Humanism is a man-centered philosophy that attempts to solve the problems of man and the world independently of God."[2] In today's world there are two major conflicting philosophies upon which we are building our lives—either the solid rock of God's Word or the shifting sands of humanism.

The foundation stone of all humanistic thought is atheism—the belief that there is no God. "As nontheists, we begin with humans, not God, nature not deity. Promises of immortal salvation or fear of eternal damnation are illusory and harmful."[3]

But God's Word declares, "The fool has said in his heart, 'There is no God'" (Ps. 14:1). But I know that my Redeemer lives. He is the Living Word of God. Jesus Christ is Lord, and He is God (see Phil. 2:6, 11; John 1:3).

Another humanist tenet proclaims that there are no absolutes when it comes to morality. "Ethics is autonomous and situational, needing no theological or ideological sanction. . . . Reason and intelligence are the most effective instruments that humankind possesses. There is no substitute, neither faith nor passion suffice in itself."[4]

God's Word says there are absolutes—unchangeable commandments—morality issued from God Himself. The Bible, however, is a book of great principles, not minute laws about each and every detail of life. God allows people to think and search for daily guidance.

The next logical conclusion for the humanist is an autonomous, self-centered man, with unlimited goodness and potential if his environment is controlled to let his free spirit develop. Francis Schaeffer pointed out that autonomous thinking historically does not lead to world betterment but to chaos. The humanists emphasize feeling rather than responsibility. The "I want my way" individual will seek to get rather than give, lust rather than love, demand rather than contribute. This all leads to hostility and war.

THE RIGHT ROLE MODELS

To correct this distorted view, mistreated woman should look to the role models God gives. First and foremost, God's Son, the Lord Jesus Christ, epitomizes the loving servant-leader-protector. We then must look at those men in whom Jesus Christ is living to see these principles practiced. No one but Jesus is perfect, but we can see His likeness shining through in men attempting to live the Spirit-filled life.

Many of the goals of the humanists are those of all mankind. They want love, peace, self-worth, provision, and protection, but they have denied and scorned the Word of God, who is infinite love and everlasting peace, the one who gives self-worth and identity, who is our Provider, Refuge, and Strength.

What is the answer to the storms of life, the swirling winds of change, the torrential rains of adversity, and the floodtides of doubt and despair? We as Christians can't deny the discrimination and abuse of the poor, women, children, and minority groups. We can't deny the problems of unwanted pregnancies, drug abuse, perversion, power-hungry men and women, and war. We can't deny that our resources are being wasted and that crime is on the upsurge. We're both afraid to stay at home and afraid to go out of our houses.

What will we Christians do? What can we offer to the world? We must build our lives and the lives of our families on the sure foundation of God's Word. We must tell our neighbors, our friends, the ungodly, yes, the humanists that the answer to the storms of life is the Word of God: JESUS—the living, powerful Word of God; THE BIBLE—the written Word of God. They are inseparable.

Being a Christian and trusting in His Word doesn't make us immune to the storms of life. I've been in the floodtides of sorrow. As the rains and winds beat upon my life, when the floods tried to overwhelm me, I held onto the Solid Rock, and my house withstood the storm.

COSTLY TRENDS

In *The Wall Street Journal* Joann S. Lublin wrote:

> Gaps are narrowing between the sexes in alcoholism, suicide, crime, and even car crashes. Some are pointing to added stresses related to female "emancipation." Federal health officials estimate that one of every three Americans with a drinking problem is a woman, compared with only one of six a decade ago.
>
> In the wake of the revolution in sex roles and gains in female employment, women are increasingly afflicted by a range of social and physical problems that used to be largely the domain of men. It is a phenomenon

that some describe—in a much-disputed analysis—as "the dark side of female emancipation."[5]

Alice Rossi, a University of Massachusetts sociology professor, says, "when you break the homebound nature of women's lives and get them into jobs, then you're bound to get an elevation of their drinking, smoking, and accident rates."[6]

Another cost of equality is the loss of femininity. In a recent article in our local newspaper the headline was "Accent Is on Management." This is what followed:

> There's only one way for women to get to the top: forget they are women. At least that's the conclusion of one woman who conducted 300 interviews for her book on working for a female boss.
>
> Trash femininity, stop baking brownies and nix plans for babies. Because the nature of leadership is unchangeable, "women must become clones of men" if they are to make it to the chief executive's suite, said author Dr. Paula Bern.
>
> "Women have to emulate the skills many see as masculine—decisiveness, aggressiveness, assertiveness and willingness to take risks," she said.
>
> Although 37 percent of the nation's managers are women, "at the top echelon, there are zero," said Dr. Bern, author of *How to Work for a Woman Boss, Even if You'd Rather Not*.[7]

The chief problem in discussing feminism, I feel, is an inability to distinguish correctly between biblical principles, sin-related abuses, and man-made customs. Biblical principles are unchanging. Sin-related abuses are always wrong, and man-made customs may be good, bad, or just outdated.

Biblical Principles

To establish biblical principles one must first determine her view of the nature of holy Scripture. Norman L. Geisler and William Nix briefly explain the three major views about the place of the Bible in God's revelation:

> The liberal view is that the Bible contains the Word of God, along with the words and errors of men. This view is based upon a naturalistic premise. It makes human reason and feeling the final judges of revelation, and it does not take seriously what the Bible has to say about itself.
>
> The neoorthodox view is that the Bible becomes the Word of God

when its message becomes meaningful to the individual. This position is too subjective. It ignores the fact that the Bible is not only a record of personal revelations, but that it is itself a propositional revelation.

The conservative view is that the Bible is the written Word of God. It holds that Bible to be God's objective revelation whether or not man has a subjective illumination of it.[8]

I subscribe to the verbal plenary inspiration concept because I believe all the words (verbal) written in the Bible are God-breathed (see 2 Tim. 3:16). God gave full expression to His thought (plenary) in the words of the biblical record. He guided in the choice of words used within the cultural context and according to the personality of the writers so that, in some inscrutable manner, the Bible is the Word of God while being the words of men.

One's view of the nature of Scripture will greatly influence the manner of her interpretation. For instance, the person who accepts verbal plenary inspiration will believe that Adam and Eve were real people who lived in the Garden of Eden, who sinned, and who were judged by God. Also, people who hold this view of Scripture will not attempt to do away with the concept of the fatherhood of God. The words are clearly male—Father, Son, He, Him.

Man-made Customs

Customs vary from age to age and from culture to culture. There are customs related to modesty, to masculinity, and to manners, as well as many other areas of life. In our culture it is considered rude to belch after you eat, but it is a sign of delight and satisfaction in Taiwan. In the Middle East a woman must cover her shoulders lest she be considered provocative. Twenty years ago in this country a man was considered "henpecked" if he helped with the dishes or changed diapers. These are culture-related customs, not great underlying principles from the Word of God.

A problem arises when customs and principles are so closely joined that it becomes difficult to separate them. Nevertheless, customs should not be lightly or suddenly laid aside.

We must have God's wisdom to be able to discern between man-made customs and biblical principles. But customs may change. In the 1960s some Christians thought it was sinful for a man's hair to go over his ears or touch his collar. Some of us were disturbed over our children conforming to the cultural change of long hair on men. Now men's hair styles are shorter.

Whereas longer hair was a symbol of rebellion in the 1960s, the skinhead is a sign of rebellion now.

Customs change. Hairstyles change. Fashions change. But God's written Word is the same, and it is as true now as it was when it was originally inspired. And Jesus Christ, the living Word, is "the same yesterday, today, and forever" (Heb. 13:8).

TYING IT ALL TOGETHER

In summary, the secret to a godly woman's influence is living under authority. Jesus gave great praise for the faith of the centurion who asked Him to heal his servant. This army officer confessed he was not worthy for Jesus to come to his house; but if He would only speak the word, his servant would be healed.

The centurion declared, "For I also am a man under authority, having soldiers under me. And I say to this one, 'Go,' and he goes; and to another, 'Come,' and he comes; and to my servant, 'Do this,' and he does it. When Jesus heard it, He marveled, and said to those who followed, 'I have not found such great faith, not even in Israel!'" (Matt. 8:10).

What was the secret of the centurion's faith? Why did Jesus commend him? The centurion understood the principle of living under authority. This principle works in every area of life. His life as a soldier operated upon this principle every day. He knew that those who *have* authority are those who *live under* authority.

He surmised that the spiritual world must work on the same principle. He had observed that Jesus had authority over sickness, so he knew Jesus was a man who lived under spiritual authority. Even so, if we as women understand the principle of living under authority, we will be women of incomparable faith, and we will exercise godly authority. But we will not have to demand our rights. Others will recognize this authority and follow the leadership of one who is living under authority.

Godly authority does not always involve having the number-one position. Many times a person with another position may have even greater ability in some areas than the head person. If he or she is not mainly interested in getting the credit and gaining recognition, even more significant influence can be exercised.

For instance, a wife can have tremendous influence on her husband's decisions if she is wise in her counsel and if she has a submissive spirit.

God has promised an appropriate recognition for her ideas. Proverbs 31:28 says, "Her children rise up and call her blessed; her husband also and he praises her."

I believe, in the long run, a wife can have more influence and know more true success in a supportive position to make her husband successful than if she tries to succeed in her own separate career.

> *Two are better than one, because they have a good reward for their labor. For if they fall, one will lift up his companion. But woe to him who is alone when he falls, for he has no one to help him up. Again, if two lie down together, they will keep warm; but how can one be warm alone? Though one may be overpowered by another, two can withstand him. And a threefold cord is not quickly broken. (Eccl. 4:9-12).*

I believe the third part of the cord that binds them together is God's precious Holy Spirit. Thank God, we can know true freedom, hope, joy, and contentment if we live under God's principle of authority. Esther risked her life to fall down before the king to intercede for the lives of her people. Because he saw in her a godly, submissive spirit, he held out the golden scepter toward her. "So Esther arose and stood before the king" (Est. 8:4). So should we come humbly before our heavenly King in quiet submission, seeking His will for our lives. When we do, God will reach out His loving hand of mercy toward us and say, "Arise, my daughter. Stand before Me, and I will grant you your request."

Notes

1 Search for a Wise Woman

1. Paul E. Adolph, *Release from Tension* (Chicago: Moody Press, 1956), p. 73.
2. *The New Scofield Reference Bible* (New York: Oxford University Press), p. 609, Psalm 19:9, footnote 2.
3. Oswald Chambers, *Still Higher for His Highest* (Fort Washington, Pa.: Christian Literature Crusade, 1934, 1970), p. 66.

2 The Wise Woman Works

1. Watchman Nee, *The Spiritual Man* (New York: Christian Fellowship Publishers, Inc., 1968), p. 1, 10.
2. J. Sidlow Baxter, *Going Deeper* (Grand Rapids, Mich.: Zondervan Publications, 1959), p. 30. Used by permission.
3. Oswald Chambers, *Still Higher for His Highest* (Fort Washington, Pa.: Christian Literature Crusade, 1934, 1970), p. 80.
4. The general concept of "spiritual contaminants" is drawn from *Release from Tension* by Paul Adolph (Chicago: Moody Press, 1956), pp. 63-136.
5. Ibid., p. 65

3 The Source of Wisdom

1. A. B. Simpson, Tract #12 (Warminster, Pa.).
2. Roy and Revel Hession, *We Would See Jesus* (Fort Washington, Pa.: Christian Literature Crusade, 1934).
3. Ibid.
4. Andrew Murray, *God's Best Secrets* (Westchester, Ill.: Good News Publishers, 1962).
5. Andrew Murray, *Abide in Christ* (Fort Washington, Pa.: Christian Literature Crusade, 1963), p. 84.
6. Quoted from a sermon.

5 Battle of Identity

1. Jack Taylor, *One Home Under God* (Nashville, Tenn.: Broadman and Holman, 1974), p. 109.
2. Tim LaHaye, *The Spirit-Controlled Temperament* (Wheaton, Ill.: Tyndale House, 1966).

8 Some Will Have Husbands

1. Larry Christenson, *The Christian Family* (Minneapolis, Minn.: Bethany Fellowship, 1970), p. 32-33.

12 Keeper at Home

1. Ella May Miller, *Contentment—Great Gain* (Virginia: Heart to Heart), pamphlet. Used by permission.
2. Ella May Miller, *A Woman in Her Home* (Chicago: Moody Press, 1968), p. 14.
3. Ibid., p. 67.

13 Feeding Her Family

1. *Nutrition Almanac* (New York: McGraw-Hill Book Co., 1975), p. 11.

14 Women in Ministry

1. Catherine Allen, *A Century to Celebrate, History of Women's Missionary Union* (Birmingham, Ala.: New Hope Press, 1987), p. 148.
2. Ibid., p. 46.
3. Ibid., p. 330.
4. Mrs. Howard Taylor, *The Triumph of John and Betty Stam* (Chicago: Moody Press, 1935), pp. 141, 143.
5. Ethel Mary Baldwin and David V. Benson, *Henrietta Mears and How She Did It!* (Glendale, Calif.: Regal Books, 1966).

17 Trends, Pressures, and Hopes

1. "Revolution: Tomorrow Is Now," Chapter Workbook, comp. Mary Samis, Tish Sommers, Marjorie Suelzle, and Nan Wood (Washington, D.C.: National Organization for Women, 1973), p. 18.
2. Tim LaHaye, *The Battle for the Mind* (Old Tappan, N.J.: Fleming Revell, 1980), p. 27.
3. Ibid., p. 57.
4. *Humanist Manifestos I and II* (Buffalo, N.Y.: Prometheus Books, 1973), p. 16.
5. "The Cost of Equality," *The Wall Street Journal*, Vol. 65, No. 9 (January 14, 1980).
6. Ibid.
7. *The Commercial Appeal*, Memphis, Tenn., July 25, 1987.
8. Norman L. Geisler and William Nix, *A General Introduction to the Bible* (Chicago: Moody Press, 1968), pp. 46-47.

Reading Lists

BOOKS ON BIBLE STUDY

Mears, Henrietta. *What the Bible Is All About*. rev. ed. Ventura, Calif.: Regal Books, 1983. (Over 4,000,000 in print—featuring Jesus in all of the Bible.)

DEVOTIONAL BOOKS

Chambers, Oswald. *The Place of Help*. Fort Washington, Pa.: Christian Literature Crusade, 1975.

_____. *Not Knowing Where*. Fort Washington, Pa.: Christian Literature Crusade, 1989.

Elliot, Elisabeth. *A Path Through Suffering*. Ann Arbor, Mich.: Servant Publications, 1990.

_____. *Discipline: The Glad Surrender*. Grand Rapids, Mich.: Fleming Revell, 1992.

_____. *Gateway to Joy*. Ann Arbor, Mich.: Servant Publications, 1998.

Hepburn, Daisy. *Forget Not His Blessings*. Nashville, Tenn.: Thomas Nelson Publishers, 1993.

Hurnard, Hannah. *Hinds' Feet on High Places*. Wheaton Ill.: Tyndale House, 1987.

Lawrence, Brother. *The Practice of the Presence of God*. Westwood, N.J.: Fleming Revell, 1958.

Moore, Beth. *Things Pondered*. Nashville, Tenn.: Broadman and Holman, 1997.

Morrissey, Lynn D., ed. *Treasures of a Woman's Heart*. Lancaster, Pa.: Starburst Publishers, 2000.

Musser, Joe, and Hefley, James and Marti. *Fire on the Hills. The Rochunga Pudaite Story*. Wheaton, Ill.: Tyndale House, 1998.

Myers, Ruth. *31 Days of Praise*. Sisters, Ore.: Multnomah Books, 1994.

Rogers, Adrian. *A Family Christmas Treasury*. Wheaton, Ill.: Crossway Books, 1997.

_____. *God's Hidden Treasures*. Wheaton, Ill.: Tyndale House, 1999.

_____. *The Lord Is My Shepherd*. Wheaton, Ill.: Crossway Books, 1999.

BOOKS FOR WOMEN

Bright, Vonette Zachary. *For Such a Time As This*. San Bernardino, Calif.: Campus Crusade for Christ, 1978.

_____, ed. *The Greatest Lesson I've Ever Learned*. Orlando, Fla.: New Life Publishers, 1990, 2000.

Briscoe, Jill. *A Woman of Substance*. Wheaton, Ill.: Victor Books, 1988.

_____. *Women in the Life of Jesus*. Wheaton, Ill.: Victor Books, 1994.

_____. *Women Who Changed Their World*. Colorado Springs, Colo.: Chariot Victor, 1991.

Dobson, James. *Emotions: Can You Trust Them?* Ventura, Calif.: Regal Books, 1981.

Elliot, Elisabeth. *Let Me Be a Woman*. Wheaton, Ill.: Tyndale House, 1976.

Foh, Susan T. *Women and the Word of God: A Response to Biblical Feminism*. Phillipsburg, N.J.: Presbyterian and Reformed, 1979.

LaHaye, Beverly. *The Spirit-Controlled Woman*. Eugene, Ore.: Harvest House Publishers, 1979.

Omartian, Stormie. *The Power of a Praying Wife*. Eugene, Ore.: Harvest House Publishers, 1997.

Patterson, Dorothy, and Kelley, Rhonda, eds. *The Woman's Study Bible*. Nashville, Tenn.: Thomas Nelson, 1995.

Wright, H. Norman. *Questions Women Ask in Private*. Ventura, Calif.: Regal Books, 1993.

BOOKS ON CHRISTIAN LIVING

Chambers, Oswald. *Prayer, A Holy Occupation*. Grand Rapids, Mich.: Discovery House Publishers, 1992.

Olford, Stephen F. *Not I, But Christ*. Wheaton, Ill.: Crossway Books, 1995.

Rogers, Adrian. *Believe in Miracles But Trust in Jesus*. Wheaton, Ill.: Crossway Books, 1997.

_____. *God's Wisdom Is Better Than Gold*. Memphis, Tenn.: Love Worth Finding Ministries, 2001.

_____. *Mastering Your Emotions*. Nashville, Tenn.: Broadman and Holman, 1988.

_____. *The Power of His Presence*. Wheaton, Ill.: Crossway Books, 1995.

BOOKS ON HOMEMAKING

Andersen, Georg, and Dean, Edith. *Interior Decorating*. Minneapolis, Minn.: Bethany House Publishers, 1983.

Aslett, Don. *The Cleaning Encyclopedia*. New York: Dell Trade Paperback, 1993.

Barnes, Emilie. *The Fifteen Minute Organizer*. Eugene, Ore.: Harvest House Publishers, 1991.

_____. *Welcome Home*. Eugene, Ore.: Harvest House Publishers, 1997.

Schaeffer, Edith. *The Hidden Art of Homemaking*. Wheaton, Ill.: Tyndale House, 1980.

BOOKS ON HOSPITALITY

Bright, Vonette. *The Joy of Hospitality*. Orlando, Fla.: New Life Publications, 1996.

Crabb, Rachael. *The Personal Touch*. Colorado Springs, Colo.: NavPress, 1990.

BOOKS ON MARRIAGE AND THE FAMILY

Brandt, Henry. *I Want My Marriage to Be Better*. Grand Rapids, Mich.: Zondervan, 1979.

Dobson, James. *Love for a Lifetime*. Sisters, Ore.: Questar Publishers, 1993.

Dobson, James. *What Wives Wish Their Husbands Knew About Women*. Wheaton, Ill.: Tyndale House, 1975.

LaHaye, Tim and Beverly. *The Act of Marriage*. Grand Rapids, Mich.: Zondervan, 1979.

_____. *Spirit-Controlled Family Living*. Old Tappan, N.J.: Fleming Revell, 1978.

Rogers, Adrian. *Ten Secrets for a Successful Family*. Wheaton, Ill.: Crossway Books, 1996.

Smalley, Gary, and Trent, John, Ph.D. *Celebrate the Family*. Wheaton, Ill.: Tyndale House, 1999.

Wheat, Ed and Gaye. *Intended for Pleasure*. Old Tappan, N.J.: Fleming Revell, 1977.

Wright, Norman. *Communication, Key to Your Marriage*. Ventura, Calif.: Gospel Light Publications, 1974.

_____. *More Communication Keys for Your Marriage*. Ventura, Calif.: Regal Books, 1984.

BOOKS ON CHILDREN

Brandt, Henry, and Landrum, Phil. *I Want to Enjoy My Children*. Grand Rapids, Mich.: Zondervan, 1979.

Campbell, Ross. *How to Really Love Your Child*. Colorado Springs, Colo.: Scripture Press Publications, 1977.

Crabb, Lawrence J. and Allender, Dan B. *Encouragement: The Key to Caring*. Grand Rapids, Mich.: Zondervan, 1984.

Dobson, James. *The New Dare to Discipline*. Wheaton, Ill.: Tyndale House, 1992.

_____. *Hide or Seek*. Old Tappan, N.J.: Fleming Revell, 1979.

_____. *The Strong-Willed Child*. Wheaton, Ill.: Tyndale House, 1985.

Elliot, Elisabeth. *Passion and Purity*. Old Tappan, N.J.: Fleming Revell, 1984.

_____. *The Shaping of the Christian Family*. Nashville, Tenn.: Oliver-Nelson Books, 1992.

Haystead, Wes. *Teaching Your Child About God*. Ventura, Calif.: Regal Books, 1995.

Hoving, Walter. *Tiffany's Table Manners for Teenagers*. New York: Random House, 1989.

LaHaye, Beverly. *Understanding Your Child's Temperament*. Eugene, Ore.: Harvest House Publishers, 1997.

Leman, Kevin. *Bringing Up Kids Without Tearing Them Down*. New York: Delacorte Press, 1993.

Meier, Paul. *Christian Child-Rearing and Personality Development*. Grand Rapids, Mich.: Baker Book House, 1977.

Patterson, Dorothy. *Where's Mom?* Wheaton, Ill.: Council for Biblical Manhood and Womanhood, 1990.

Reisser, Paul C., and Focus on the Family Physicians Resource Council. *Complete Book of Baby and Child Care*. Wheaton, Ill.: Tyndale House, 1997.

BOOKS ON NUTRITION

Balch, James F., M. D., and Balch, Phyliss A., C.N.C. *Prescription for Nutritional Healing*. Garden City Park, N.Y.: Avery Publishing, 1997.

Baxter, J. Sidlow. *Our High Calling*. Grand Rapids, Mich.: Zondervan, 1967.

Bragg, Paul, N.D., Ph.D. *Apple Cider Vinegar*. Santa Barbara, Calif.: Health Science.

_____. *The Shocking Truth About Water*. Desert Hot Springs, Calif.: Health Science, 1976.

Cooper, Dr. Kenneth H. *Fit Kids*. Nashville, Tenn.: Broadman and Holman, 1999.

Crook, William G., M.D. *The Yeast Connection*. Jackson, Tenn.: Professional Books, 1989.

Elwood, Cathryn. *Feel Like a Million*. New York: Pocket Books, 1956.

Duffy, William. *Sugar Blues*. Denver, Colo.: The Nutri-Books Corp., 1975.

Frahm, Anne E., with Frahm, David J. *A Cancer Battle Plan*. Colorado Springs, Colo.: Piñon, 1993.

Josephson, Elmer. *God's Key to Health and Happiness*. Grand Rapids, Mich.: Fleming Revell, 1998.

Kirschman, John D. *Nutrition Almanac*. New York: McGraw-Hill Book Co., 1975.

McMillen, S. I. *None of These Diseases*. Old Tappan, N.J.: Fleming Revell, 1963.

Nichols, Joe, and Presley, James. *"Please, Doctor, Do Something!"* Old Greenwich, Connecticut: Devin-Adair Co., 1972.

Reichenberg-Ullman, Judyth, N.D., M.S.W., and Ullman, Robert, N.D. *Ritalin-Free Kids*. Rocklin, Calif.: Prima Health, 1996.

Rogers, Joyce. *The Bible's Seven Secrets to Healthy Eating*. Wheaton, Ill.: Crossway Books, 2001.

Russell, Rex, M. D. *What the Bible Says About Healthy Living*. Ventura, Calif.: Regal Books, 1996.